JACKIE

LIFE AND STYLE OF JACQUELINE KENNEDY ONASSIS

Text
Chiara Pasqualetti Johnson

Editorial Project
Valeria Manferto De Fabianis

Editorial Assistant
Giorgio Ferrero

Graphic Layout
Maria Cucchi

JACKIE

LIFE AND STYLE OF JACQUELINE KENNEDY ONASSIS

WHITE STAR PUBLISHERS

Contents

Jacqueline Bouvier Kennedy photographed by Jacques Lowe in Hyannis Port in the summer of 1960. A few months later she would become First Lady of the United States of America, aged just 31.

Introduction

Beautiful, cultured, refined. A true queen, capable of earning the respect of the powerful and touching the hearts of the people. One can count on the fingers of one hand the women who are unquestionably considered style icons, those who provoke not debate but simply concurring opinions. One of them is Jackie. Admired, emulated, and never forgotten. Her existence spanned the twentieth century, bequeathing to history the image of an intelligent, determined woman with inimitable charisma and *savoir faire*. Discreet but seductive, she lived a fate marked by fortune, success, social stardom, and grief. Fragile and sensitive, she was forced to brace herself for the harsh trials that life placed before her. Shy and reserved, she was doomed to forever be in the spotlight, elegant and beautiful, smiling amiably in front of every camera lens. She was portrayed in thousands of photographs, yet she always remained an enigmatic, elusive soul. After all, as actress Natalie Portman, who played her in the biopic *Jackie,* said, "Every person is a mystery, but she is a bigger mystery than most." For Jackie, things were never exactly as they appeared. She had the ability to shape reality to her imagination from the time she was a child. Jacqueline Lee Bouvier grew up idealizing the charms of an unhinged father who instilled in her the idea of a femininity full of charm, elegance, and reserve. Meanwhile, her mother constantly advised her "Darling, you must not appear more intelligent than the men you meet, otherwise you will frighten them." Girls like her were brought up to aspire to a successful marriage and become perfect wives, a model of womanhood far removed from Jackie's ambitions, who from a young age knew exactly what she wanted and how to get it. She took her first step toward it at eighteen, crossing the ocean to study in Paris. By the time she returned, she had grown into a charming young lady with an unconventional but irresistible beauty. Athletic and lithe, she had none of the velvety softness or buttery femininity of Marilyn Monroe. But she possessed personality, charisma, good taste, and a mastery of the media, learned while working as a photojournalist for the Washington *Times-Herald.*

A portrait from the early 1960s in perfect "Jackie style," featuring an Oleg Cassini suit and matching pillbox hat, three strings of pearls, and her unmistakable smile.

Only this explosive mix of grace and vitality could have handled such a complicated chemistry with John Fitzgerald Kennedy, making her the only possible companion for the future President of the United States of America. In the history of First Ladies, there is a before and there is an after. The watershed date is January 20, 1961, when Jacqueline entered the White House alongside her husband. From that moment on, nothing was ever the same. The expression "power couple" was in fact born with them: no one else had so perfectly embodied their captivating glamour, telegenic appeal and charm on a global scale, balancing the precarious equilibrium between public and private life. First Lady for only three years, Jackie quickly learned to navigate life alongside a man who was almost always absent, often ill, and perpetually unfaithful. A handful of public outings was all she needed to conquer the world. Subtle but never boring, elegant but with a dash of flair and the epitome of sophistication, the unforgettable "Jackie style" sparked, indeed set ablaze, the fashion trends of yesterday and today. Every element of her wardrobe represents a timeless classic; and ever since, those looks have been constantly replicated, endlessly reflecting the image of the woman who made them immortal, transcending the scrutiny of the society she seduced. Decades later, the legend that is Jackie continues to fuel a common imagination literally bewitched by a figure so iconic and yet so contemporary that she inspired designers and actresses, but also many of us. She became a star from her first appearance on the cover of *Life* magazine in 1953, on the occasion of her engagement. From that moment, women all over the world admired her in the outfits that designer Oleg Cassini created especially for her, or in the stunning evening gowns designed by Balenciaga and Givenchy. They may seem frivolous; but behind those choices was always great consistency and a willingness to use fashion to make a statement, communicating a very specific message to those who were watching her. Like when she chose to wear the fiery red suit that matched the uniforms of the Royal Canadian Mounted Police for her first official visit, the apricot-colored silk worn as a tribute to the colors of India, and even the refined haute couture creations in which she appeared in the presence of Charles de Gaulle. And of course, the unforgettable pink suit she wore on November 22, 1963, in Dallas, which she would keep on, bloodstained, until the next morning. From that day, she learned to carry the burden of others' judgment, enduring the changing feelings of a nation that would not always be sympathetic to her. In the eyes of the world she was no longer just a woman, but the very symbol of her own suffering. Having shifted from being idolized to stigmatized, she defied public opinion by marrying Aristotle Onassis. After all, she had always been attracted to strong, powerful men, capable of taking risks in order to succeed, but inexorably destined to overshadow her intellectual abilities, stifling the true ambitions of a personality as complex as Jackie's. "I realize now that I can't do it anymore," she revealed when she was widowed for the second time. With her three lives, the first as Jacqueline Bouvier, the second as Jackie Kennedy, and the third as Jackie O, she proved that nothing could destroy her. She regained public legitimacy with a career in publishing and by committing herself to the defense of historic monuments: healing, however imperfectly and incompletely, in front of the nation's eyes. "There are two kinds of women: those who want power in the world, and those who want power in bed," she said when she introduced herself to Maurice Tempelsman, the man with whom she would share the later part of her life before passing away, with him at her side, in 1994. Universally admired and astonishingly fascinating, she is still considered one of the most mysterious souls of all time. Who really was the only queen America ever had? Beyond the style, beyond the glory, behind the famous last names that marked the course of her existence was her. Quite simply, Jackie.

"I want
to live my life,
not record it."

*Jackie aged 30 in one of her most famous
photographs, taken in Hyannis Port in August 1959.*

An American in Paris (1929–1950)

Jacqueline Bouvier was always top of the class. At five years old, she could already read and rode her pony like a champion, then went to study in Paris. She became a beautiful debutante with a Mona Lisa smile, a head full of dreams, and one absolute certainty: she would never become "just a housewife."

Photographed beside her pony in perfect equestrian garb, five-year-old Jacqueline, with her natural charm and princess-worthy upbringing, already possessed the class of a lady. Indeed, she had the expectations of two great New York families placed on her shoulders from the day she was born. Her mother, Janet Lee, was an educated and brilliant young woman, distantly related to the Rockefellers and the Vanderbilts and engaged in an ambitious social climb to access the elite of American high society. She knew that neither the wealth her family had accumulated through her father's enormous real estate investments, nor her prestigious studies or perfect French, would be enough; what she really needed was a good match. She seized her chance in 1928, when she married John Vernou Bouvier III, one of New York's most coveted bachelors. Tall and muscular, he was the runaway heir to a wealthy family that continued to support him despite his dissolute lifestyle. After being expelled from college for organizing illicit games of poker, he graduated from Yale and then began a career as a stockbroker on Wall Street. With his rogue yet endearing manners, he had the irresistible charm of a Hollywood actor and looked so much like Clark Gable that he used to get mobbed by autograph-hunting fans.

Little Jacqueline with her pony in August 1934, during the Southampton Riding and Hunt Club's riding competition on Long Island.

He wore tailored suits with wide lapels to enhance his athletic physique, paired with handmade two-tone shoes that added a dandy-esque touch to the ensemble. Friends nicknamed him "Black Jack," perhaps because of his exotic, tan complexion, or more likely due to his unbridled passion for cards that would soon lead to his downfall. Indifferent to his playboy reputation, young Janet became bewitched by this irresistible man who was sixteen years her senior. After a brief engagement, the wedding was celebrated at a prestigious East Hampton country club with a select group of guests consisting of bankers, lawyers, and stockbrokers. As soon as they were married, the Bouviers moved into a luxurious love nest made available to the couple by Janet's father: an eleven-room apartment overlooking Park Avenue.

Their firstborn daughter, Jacqueline Lee Bouvier, was born in Southampton on July 28, 1929. She was given a double surname, her mother's and father's, and was baptized according to the Catholic Rite at the Church of St. Ignatius Loyola in New York City. A few months later, the excitement over the child's arrival was overshadowed by the black cloud of the Wall Street crash that dragged the Bouviers into a storm. Black Jack's precarious wealth suffered a devastating collapse, from which he was only able to emerge thanks to his wife's substantial assets that allowed him to continue living well above his means. His brazen opulence was even reported in the society gossip columns of the newspaper, in the detailed account of little Jacqueline's social debut at the lavish party held in honor of her second birthday.

A family photo with her father John Vernou Bouvier III, known as "Black Jack," and mother Janet Lee in the summer of 1934.

But behind the façade of a seemingly comfortable life, the atmosphere grew increasingly tense, and it was only the arrival of a second daughter, Caroline, affectionately known as Lee, that saved the couple—their relationship now in shambles because of Black Jack's constant drinking and escapades—from imminent divorce.

Unaware of his shortcomings, Jacqueline showed a deep attachment to her father from an early age. Not only had she inherited the nickname Jackie, a feminized version of her father's name, but she looked very much like him. They shared the same high cheekbones, skin tone, and strong-willed nature, as well as a taste for beauty and a natural inclination toward elegance. He was rarely present during the winter season, and the little girl looked forward to vacations, where he'd take her swimming in the ocean. Idealizing those memories, Jackie would chase a lifelong dream of recreating the lost paradise of her childhood years and summers spent with her parents at Lasata, the Bouvier family's summer residence. Spread across seven acres, it housed a tennis court,

Janet Lee Bouvier and her daughter Jacqueline photographed at the family estate in East Hampton.

riding stables, and a charming garden with an Italian-style fountain filled with goldfish. During those idyllic vacations, little Jacqueline's paternal grandfather loved to take her to equestrian competitions, in which she soon began to participate with great success. Highly educated and a classical scholar, the Bouvier progenitor flaunted a presumed aristocratic origin, so much so that he wanted to put in writing an account of the family's social rise. He published at his own expense a book, *Our Forebears,* in which he described the Bouviers as "an ancient house of Fontaine near Grenoble." The text even reconstructed an imaginary genealogy, complete with heraldry and noble titles. The reality was quite different, and the only plausible figure in that fanciful reconstruction was the first American ancestor, Michel Bouvier. A veteran of Napoleon's army, he arrived in Philadelphia in 1817 as a cabinetmaker and then built a solid career through speculation on the coal market. Beyond the prominence, real or assumed, of the family name, Black Jack now had little else to offer his wife.

At age six, with her younger sister Lee and their bull terrier during a dog show.

17

A lover of nature, Jackie adored dogs from an early age. On the left, a picture taken when she was six years old in 1935. In the photo above, she smiles next to Great Dane King Phar at the Long Island Kennel Club dog show in Hewlett Harbor.

More concerned about the money he was losing at the poker table than the catastrophic stock market bulletins, he was up to his neck in debt. Seemingly unworried about the decline of his fortune, he spoiled the girls with unexpected gifts and fashionable clothes, taking them with him on daring expeditions to casinos and racetracks, where he made sure they were always noticed for their elegance. Soon, however, tensions between the Bouviers came to a climax, and the couple finally hit a crisis point following resounding allegations of infidelity that were picked up by the tabloids.

Humbled by the scandal of the revelations splashed across the papers, Janet's only satisfaction came from raising her daughters. The path laid out for them included good manners, beautiful but traditional clothing, and a demure femininity coupled with healthy athletic vigor. As disciplined as soldiers, they received from their mother what she believed to be the necessary lessons to transform them into two women at least as ambitious as herself. "Do you know the secret to being happy and content?" she once asked her daughters during teatime. "Money and power." Each in her own way, both Bouvier sisters would treasure this maternal precept.

Wearing their perfect equestrian garb, Janet Lee Bouvier and her daughter receive the Family Class trophy at the East Hampton Horse Show on August 14, 1937. On the opposite page, Jacqueline watches the races while sitting on the fence.

Janet chose an exclusive school in Manhattan for the girls, the Miss Chapin School, where she herself had studied. The very high tuition fees, the equivalent of the average American's annual salary, were paid by Grandpa Bouvier. He loved his granddaughters and was well aware of how important a girl's "pedigree" was. A suitable course of study and friendships were indispensable, not to build a professional résumé, but to catch a husband. "The women of my generation," Jackie would one day say, "weren't meant to have careers. We were raised for marriage." Her mother Janet was more aware of this than anyone else, and as soon as the inevitable divorce from Black Jack was signed in 1940, she devoted herself diligently to the search for a new husband. A year later, she made official her relationship with Hugh Dudley Auchincloss Jr., a multimillionaire banker and heir to Standard Oil, unattractive but extremely rich, posh and sober. He too was fresh from not one but two divorces, including one from Nina Gore, the mother of writer Gore Vidal. Jackie was asked to call him "Uncle Hughdie" from the day they moved from New York to his stately home in Virginia, one of the most lavish in the United States. Merrywood was a Georgian mansion with gardens overlooking the Potomac River. Its grounds housed a swimming pool, stables, and tennis courts, perfect for developing Jackie's athletic aptitudes. In that gilded sanctuary, she tolerated without too much jealousy the birth of her two half-siblings, Janet and Jamie. In the summer, the family moved to the second Auchincloss family home, Hammersmith Farm in Newport, where Jacqueline and her sister had a wonderful time, though they always felt they were mere guests of their stepfather's, who never showed much generosity to his new wife's daughters.

Dressed in her riding habit, nine-year-old Jackie was already showing off her innate elegance and irresistible smile.

In spite of the splendor of that luxurious estate, Jackie would return to her father as soon as she could, who, in the meantime, had moved to a small apartment in Manhattan. He would serve her dinner by setting up a small folding table in front of the fireplace, then turn the living room into a bedroom for her. In the summer he would rent a small cottage on the beach, where his daughters would join him full of anticipation for the days they would spend together, with no regrets for their lost luxuries. The unconditional love of that reckless father was joyfully reciprocated by the girls, who mirrored his adoring gaze. He would be the one to instill in Jacqueline her idea of femininity, which was a combination of charm, elegance, and reserve. "When you smile, think of Leonardo's *Mona Lisa,*" he would repeat to her like a mantra, revealing the secret to pressing her full lips into a reassuring, measured smile, an expression destined to make Jacqueline's stunning face even more charming.

Behind that apparent grace lay a determined character, tempered by the pain of her parents' separation, which occurred at a time when divorce still represented a stigma that cast a shadow over the children of separated couples. It was the first setback in an almost perfect childhood. Aged eleven, that heartbreak forced her to face a harsh reality and made Jacqueline quieter and more introverted. She built a wall around herself, learning to hide her suffering behind a smile. She observed events without getting emotionally involved, concentrating on her studies and excelling due to her brilliant intelligence. Judged by her teachers as too spirited but extremely gifted, Jackie was always at the top of her class. Extremely precocious, she loved to read from a very young age. "My idols were Byron, Mowgli, Robin Hood, Little Lord Fauntleroy, and Scarlett O'Hara," she would recall many years later. She did not yet have the beauty that maturity would bring, but she stood out among her classmates. Taller than average, she complained of having a sturdy frame, hands and feet that were too big, broad shoulders and ample hips, as well as a head of untamed frizzy hair with too low a hairline, inherited from her father, which she gathered in thick brown braids. "I hated dolls, loved horses and dogs, and had skinned knees and braces on my teeth for what must have seemed like an interminable period of time to my family," she recalled.

Jacqueline on her tenth birthday with her dog Tammy at a charity event to support the Ladies Village Improvement Society.

With a view to attending one of America's top universities, at the age of fifteen she was sent to study at the exclusive Miss Porter's School in Connecticut. It would be her stepping stone into high society. Three years later, eighteen-year-old Jackie was being inundated with invitations, effortlessly navigating the whirlwind of lavish parties that were the talk of the debutante season. She was pictured among the branches of a weeping willow at the Tuxedo Autumn Ball, then photographed with carnations at the Grosvenor Ball and amid the artificial flowers that decorated the Junior Assembly ballroom. The season culminated with an event arranged for her by her mother: a tea dance for three hundred guests at the Auchincloss estate in Newport. It was her first social triumph. That year, she was crowned "Queen Debutante of the Year" for being poised, soft-spoken, and intelligent. In the New York *Journal-American* she was described as "a regal brunette who has classic features and the daintiness of Dresden porcelain" by influential journalist Igor Cassini, who signed his articles under the pseudonym Cholly Knickerbocker. He was the brother of Oleg, the designer destined to cross paths with the future First Lady. That evening was the first in a series of occasions in which Jackie distinguished herself with a sense of style that would be enormously helpful when making her entrance into the jet set. Although shy and introverted, she knew how to attract attention and never went unnoticed. "Jacqueline Bouvier is besieged by requests of all kinds, from interviews to photoshoots, but her conservative family shuns publicity," legendary American journalist Elsa Maxwell wrote of her at the time. She became a girl of icy charm who attracted every gaze, even though her body did not exactly reflect the feminine standards of the time. She was tall, thin, and agile, and, perhaps because of this, managed to embody a more modern ideal of beauty that was never vulgar. She wore simple dresses and sporty outfits, her whole look enhanced by a fresh, natural face without a trace of makeup.

Crowned Queen Debutante, at eighteen Jackie's striking beauty hinted at an already well-defined personality and a very unique look.

But the epitome of her charm, the thing that had everyone enchanted, was her barely-there smile. With her flowing gowns and elegant poise, she certainly didn't go unnoticed at receptions. She was presented to suitors as a wealthy debutante, but the reality was quite different. The means provided for the Bouvier sisters by their stepfather were limited, and his enormous wealth would never pass to them. Jackie's father did what he could, striving to maintain the role of the generous parent by bestowing a weekly allowance on the girls and providing for a portion of the school fees that, over time, became increasingly onerous. After graduation in 1947, Jackie was in fact accepted by Vassar College, the women's equivalent of Yale and Harvard. That kind of education was aimed at a new generation of women, destined to assume a prominent role in society. Jackie had chosen it for that very reason, even though for most of her classmates the goal to get married, have children, and stay at home still remained. "I don't think I ever felt as isolated as I did at Vassar," she admitted when thinking back on those years. She shared a room with Nancy L. Tuckerman, known as Tucky, who would become her personal secretary at the White House. To broaden her horizons, Jackie contributed to the school newspaper, writing articles and drawing comic strips. But above all, she dreamed of visiting Paris. The allure of the Bouviers' distant European origins fascinated Jacqueline, who liked to Frenchify the pronunciation of her name by introducing herself as "Jack-e-leen" and often used French words, beginning with the name she chose for her horse, Danseuse. Soon, to her delight, she would have the chance to immerse herself in the culture to which she felt so akin. For affluent American girls, European travel was an essential part of their education.

In 1947 she posed beside her father at the graduation ceremony at Miss Porter's School. The pair both had class and an innate sense of style, and were very close to each other.

And so the year of her debut in society coincided with Jackie's first extraordinary opportunity to visit England, Italy, Switzerland, and, of course, France. In the summer of 1948, with a small group of friends accompanied by a chaperone, she spent seven weeks visiting castles, churches, and museums, culminating with a reception in the gardens of Buckingham Palace, where she shook hands with Winston Churchill, standing in line twice so she could see him again. Upon her return home, all she wanted was another chance to relive that formidable experience.

Jackie's busy social life was punctuated by parties and balls. Above, she poses with Sloan Simpson and actress Celeste Holm at the Bal de la Soie at the Waldorf Astoria. On the left, she is pictured in a group photo during the same evening.

It is not hard to imagine her excitement when, as a reward for excellent conduct, she was granted permission to return to Europe to spend her junior year in France, a privilege granted only to a very few select female students. She left New York aboard the ocean liner *De Grasse* in August 1949, stopping in Grenoble to take a six-week intensive French language course before moving to the capital. In Paris, her mother had arranged for her to stay with a family appropriate to her rank, entrusting her to a widowed noblewoman, the Countess de Renty. The dinner conversations were intelligent and often concerned the political events of the recent past, the complex political handling of World War II and the future of France. For Jackie, those evenings would become a better education than any history course taken in American colleges could have been. Six months after her arrival in France, she was mastering the language and roaming the city with ease. She attended French history classes at the Sorbonne and art classes at the Louvre, but most of all she indulged in a busy social life, dining at the Ritz and then ending her evenings at jazz clubs. She would spend hours browsing antique stores and lurking in cafes such as Café de Flore or Les Deux Magots, hoping to catch a glimpse of Camus or Sartre. During that time she also experienced the excitement of first love, consummated in the shadow of the Eiffel Tower with the son of a French diplomat. That Parisian interlude remained etched in her memory as "the most intense moment, the happiest and most carefree year of my life." Before returning to the United States, she spent a few days traveling between Vienna and Munich. The war had ended only four years before, and the cities still bore the marks of the bombings when she visited Dachau, the concentration camp recently turned into a memorial that made a deep impression on her.

Once back home, she chose to attend her senior year at George Washington University, majoring in French literature and taking courses in creative writing and journalism. She was twenty-one years old and, by the standards of her social environment, should have already been thinking about marriage.

Jacqueline with friends on the deck of the ocean liner De Grasse *en route to France in August 1949.*

Many of her friends had already announced their engagements. But not Jackie. She missed the freedom of the year she had spent in France, so did everything she could to go back. The right opportunity presented itself unexpectedly, in the form of a contest. Putting her writing skills to good use, she won *Vogue*'s Prix de Paris, a competition for young journalists that would secure her a six-month contract as an editorial assistant in the magazine's Paris headquarters and as many months in the Manhattan office. Her winning entry was an article entitled *People I Wish I Had Known,* beating more than a thousand applicants. The text was accompanied by an eloquent self-portrait. "I am tall, 5'7", with brown hair, a square face and eyes so unfortunately far apart that it takes three weeks to have a pair of glasses made with a bridge wide enough to fit over my nose. I do not have a sensational figure but can look slim if I pick the right clothes." When they announced the winner, Jackie was over the moon, but her mother adamantly opposed the idea of her moving to Europe. Thus, she wrote to the judges that she had already spent a year in Paris and that her family was "tenaciously determined to keep me at home." To console her for that forfeit, Janet agreed to grant her a short trip to Europe with her sister Lee, who was eager to admire the wonders Jackie had described to her. That summer they boarded an ocean liner for a memorable vacation. The itinerary included Tuscany and Venice where, thanks to letters of introduction from the Auchincloss family, the Bouvier sisters were the guests of dukes and countesses. They also had the opportunity to attend art history lectures by critic Bernard Berenson and singing lessons with Puccini's favorite soprano, Gilda Dalla Rizza. By the time she returned from that trip, the child prodigy who amazed spectators by winning trophies at horse shows had become a glamorous, fashionable young lady. She did not yet know what path her life would take, but of one thing she was absolutely certain, so much so that she wrote it clearly in her profile in the school yearbook: "My life's ambition is to not be a housewife." She kept her promise.

Jacqueline and her sister Lee in September 1951.

The Wedding of the Year (1950–1952)

As a photojournalist on the streets of Washington, Jackie interviewed a variety of ordinary people and rising politicians, including one John Fitzgerald Kennedy. Both beautiful, ambitious and successful people, they were already America's most glamorous couple when their wedding day arrived, an event that would mark the beginning of an unbreakable bond made of love, politics, and style.

On a windy spring day, Jackie was hurrying through the streets of Washington. She had an appointment to interview and photograph a young Democratic congressman from Massachusetts who had recently been elected to the U.S. Congress. That meeting would change the course of her life, unexpectedly turning the plans she had made for the future on their head. After finishing college, she thought her path would be journalism, so she got a job as a photojournalist with the Washington *Times-Herald*. For $25 a week she was the editor of a column called "Inquiring Camera Girl." The assignment was to interview citizens from all walks of life, photographing them with a Graflex Speed Graphic, the bulky camera provided by the newsroom that she always carried over her shoulder.

In addition to a cast of eccentric characters, clowns and truck drivers, she interviewed Pat Nixon, the wife of the Vice President, and the First Lady's granddaughters, Ellen and Mamie Moore. She also managed to ask a few questions of a charming, blue-eyed politician with an irresistible smile who was successfully navigating the impervious roads of the political realm. He had recently been voted America's most eligible bachelor, besting even movie star Rock Hudson, while the Washington *Post* referred to him as "the most handsome congressman." His name was John Fitzgerald Kennedy.

A photojournalist for the Washington Times-Herald, *Jackie poses with her Speed Graphic camera in 1953.*

Jackie teased him by asking "Why should a happy bachelor get married?", and mocked his romantic exploits with questions such as "Do you agree that the Irish are unskilled in the art of love?" and, naïvely, "If you were dating Marilyn Monroe, what would you talk about?" This was not the first time their eyes had met. When Jackie was still attending college, he had noticed the charming Queen Debutante and flirted discreetly with her, to no avail. After all, by that time Jackie's heart was already taken. During one of the countless parties she attended, she had met John Husted Jr., a 24-year-old broker who, after graduating from Yale, was working on Wall Street. Usually cautious, Jackie had let herself get carried away. Amid a snowfall on the streets of New York City, she had accepted the marriage proposal of the boy she had met just a month earlier. He sealed the promise by giving her a precious heirloom ring of sapphires and diamonds that Jackie proudly wore. On January 21, 1952, the *Times-Herald* announced their engagement. The wedding was scheduled for June, but things did not go as planned. Janet immediately objected to the marriage, which did not live up to the aspirations she had for her daughter. "She must have fallen off her horse and hit her head," was her comment when she learned of the salary of the groom-to-be. Jackie was worth much more. The breakup happened on a March weekend when she returned the engagement ring, slipping it into Husted's pocket and confessing to him that she felt trapped in the relationship. And so this wrong John was dismissed without regret, while on the horizon loomed the right John, who had two last names: Fitzgerald-Kennedy.

On the roof of the Washington Times-Herald *building, Jackie photographs her friend Dale Chestnut feeding a goldfish.*

For that young and perpetually boyish politician, life was quickly changing, and he announced his intention to run for the Senate. It was up to him to raise the banner of his ambitious family after the tragic death of his older brother Joe, who died during World War II while flying a bomber over the skies of England. John, whom everyone in the family called Jack, was the second son of the large Kennedy family. After him came Rosemary, the most beautiful and unfortunate of them all, destined to spend much of her life interned in an institution for the mentally ill following a lobotomy. The younger siblings were Kathleen, Eunice, Patricia, Robert—called Bobby, Jean Ann, and finally Edward, nicknamed Ted. Pushing the children to the heights of politics was the unscrupulous patriarch, Joe Kennedy. In order to secure boundless wealth and power for his family, he reputedly never hesitated in making deals with gangsters and Mafiosi. While his substantial fortune was certainly enough to allow his son to finance his run for power, it was Jack's bachelorhood that threatened to be a hindrance to his political career. It was imperative that he marry as soon as possible, if only to clear his playboy reputation. And that he marry the right woman, at least in terms of appearance. "It doesn't matter who you really are; the only thing that matters is who people think you are," Joe repeated to his children.

The meeting that ignited the spark between Jackie and Jack did not happen by accident. It was arranged by Pulitzer Prize-winning journalist Charles Bartlett and his wife Martha, who engineered a romantic rendezvous, inviting the pair to their home for dinner. They liked each other immediately. "I'd never met anyone like her," Kennedy would admit in an interview with the Washington *Post* many years later. Over the course of the evening, he had watched in admiration as the young woman, so composed and full of charm, succumbed to Charles's heroic tales of his wartime service, when he had survived by swimming five hours in the ocean and staying for days on a deserted island waiting for rescue.

Senator John Fitzgerald Kennedy in a portrait taken in his Senate office shortly after announcing his engagement to Jacqueline Bouvier.

In addition to a sportsman's temperament, Jack had a good education and excellent connections with the European aristocracy, cultivated by his father when he was ambassador to Britain and strengthened by the marriage of one of his sisters to the heir to a Duchy in Devonshire. But above all, he was swaggering, maverick, and unpredictable, just like Black Jack. Jackie wanted to introduce her sweetheart to her father right away, at a dinner in New York where the two got along wonderfully, sharing the same passions for sports, politics, and women. Much more alike than they could have imagined, the baton of Jackie's heart was passed from one to the other.

When it was Jack's turn to reveal to his family that he had fallen in love with Jacqueline, the far-sighted and calculating Joe Kennedy immediately agreed. Marrying her would mean his son would have a glamorous woman at his side who would associate the family with the luster of Newport, a place of social standing that Jackie belonged to thanks to her mother's second marriage, into the Auchincloss family, and one that the patriarch fervently desired for his boy. He was enchanted by Jackie's European allure and irreverent spirit.

The full Kennedy clan. From left to right, eldest son Joseph Jr., standing behind little Robert and Edward, John Fitzgerald Kennedy next to his father Joseph Sr. and mother Rose in the center, with Jean and Patricia next to sister Eunice, seated. At right, Kathleen and Rosemary.

He saw in that refined young lady, so un-American in her manners, the ideal wife for his son. So he welcomed her graciously into the tumultuous Kennedy clan. They all lived together in a big house, full of athletic and competitive brothers and sisters who engaged in fierce baseball games and came and went from distant schools, universities, travels, and wars. "They were like carbonated water: stimulating, open, approachable," Jackie would later describe them. Her mother Janet also approved of the union.

Considering the family's power and wealth, Kennedy was undoubtedly one of the most coveted bachelors in the United States. With that engagement, she felt she had fulfilled her duty as a mother: to make of her daughters two model wives, pushing them into successful marriages that would provide them with economic stability and social status. Jackie had already agreed to Jack's proposal when she caught the bridal bouquet of her sister, Lee, the first of the two to tie the knot with the man who seemed the perfect match for her ambitions: Michael Canfield, son of the owner of the Harper & Row publishing house.

An intense portrait of Jackie. Around her neck she wears one of her favorite jewels, the three-strand pearl necklace that she will wear throughout her life.

Ahead of the wedding, Jackie resigned from the *Times-Herald,* but not before submitting her last report from Great Britain. It was on the subject of Queen Elizabeth II's coronation and made the front page. Jack immediately sent her a telegram, "Excellent article but I miss you," followed by a romantic transatlantic phone call. Shortly after her return from London, the engagement was officially announced, celebrated with a lavish reception. The sun shone that June day in 1953 on the vast grounds of Hyannis Port, the Kennedys' magnificent summer residence on Cape Cod, where the Massachusetts peninsula slashes like a hook into the Atlantic Ocean. The union was announced to a hundred or so invited guests, including renowned industrialists and high-ranking politicians, excited to pay their respects to the beautiful, young, and successful couple. The bride-to-be sported an engagement ring designed especially for her by Van Cleef & Arpels, consisting of a 2.88-carat diamond and a 2.84-carat emerald, modeled after the famous Toi-et-Moi chosen by Napoleon to propose to his wife Joséphine, with two precious gems set side by side to symbolize two souls becoming one. Many images exist of that happy day, and of the weeks that followed the announcement. While Jackie had been obliged to use the same photograph from her previous engagement to John Husted for the publication of the nuptial announcement in the newspapers, a plethora of new portraits began to circulate from that moment on. The Kennedy estate became the backdrop for a series of iconic images taken by photographers hired by patriarch Joe.

Jackie and her future husband photographed at the Kennedy estate in Hyannis Port, Massachusetts, shortly after the announcement of their engagement.

The bride-to-be already carried that irresistible mix of respectability and elegance that would constitute the essence of the "Jackie style," destined to influence fashion for decades. Radiant and perfectly cast for the role, she had a vaguely mysterious air and a sophisticated allure. She was photographed with Jack's sisters, Eunice and Jean, playing softball with the Kennedy brothers, and even barefoot on the porch. But the most famous shot is still that of the smiling couple, their hair tousled in the wind as they sail on the *Victura,* the sailboat Jack had received from his father for his fifteenth birthday. The shot was published on the cover of *Life* magazine, with the headline "Senator Kennedy Goes A-Courting." Inside, a four-page feature celebrated the engagement of the "most handsome U.S. Senator," in love and happy. In reality, just as copies of the magazine were being pored over by millions of Americans, Jack was traveling in the south of France in the company of Swedish 21-year-old Gunilla von Post, to whom he declared that if only he had met her sooner, he would have called off the engagement.

*One of the couple's most famous portraits, taken in June 1953 aboard the Kennedys'
sailboat.*

"You have to be doing something you enjoy. That is the definition of happiness!"

Happy and in love, Jackie and Jack relax on the beach, photographed by Hyman Peskin.

Athletic and competitive, the Kennedys competed in all kinds of sports. In this photo, they involve Jackie in one of their baseball games.

Jackie plays football with her future husband and his brother Bobby during a vacation at the Kennedy summer estate.

"I like men with funny noses, stick-out ears, crooked teeth. Most of all, they must have a joyful spirit."

One of the shots taken for Life magazine in 1953, accompanying the article devoted to Kennedy's engagement to Jacqueline Bouvier.

But by then there was no more room for second thoughts. Everything was now ready for "the wedding of the year," as it was immediately dubbed by the newspapers. The wedding was set for September 12, and everyone expected a memorable event. No one was disappointed. An exemplary ceremony, a regal reception, a dream wedding dress: everything seemed to border on perfection in what is still considered one of the most successful weddings ever. Jackie would have liked an intimate ceremony, with only a few guests, but her father-in-law was of a different opinion. Joe Kennedy wanted a sensational event for his son, with unprecedented media coverage. So in addition to the bride's relatives and the entire very large Kennedy clan, also attending the ceremony was the elite of American society, 800 very select guests that included bankers, millionaires, aristocrats, and tycoons. The crowd of senators, diplomats, and prominent socialites was later joined by another 400 guests who were invited to the lavish reception at Hammersmith House, the stunning estate of Jackie's stepfather Hugh D. Auchincloss. Unsurprisingly, it was on his arm that she walked down the aisle, instead of her father's. There was mention of a flu, but the truth was that Black Jack had drunk too much that morning, overwhelmed by the prospect of having to face the scrutiny of all those guests. St. Mary's Church in Newport, a place much loved by the young couple, had been chosen for the religious ceremony. As the Los Angeles *Times* reported, Jack and Jackie loved spending weekends in that quiet corner of Rhode Island. It was not difficult to run into them on Sundays at church, sitting close together, always in the tenth row. *Life* magazine reported that during the wedding mass, Cardinal Cushing, then the archbishop of Boston, celebrated the wedding rites with solemnity, referring to a "special blessing from the Pope." The bride and groom smiled radiantly as they exited the church surrounded by a dozen bridesmaids, Jack in an impeccable morning suit with a white flower in his boutonniere, and Jackie in a sumptuous gown that suited her well, even though she had not chosen it.

The official wedding dress photo. Jackie's sumptuous gown was designed by African American designer Ann Lowe.

She would have preferred something more sophisticated and modern, but a more traditional design, strongly desired by her omnipresent mother and endorsed by the opinion of her all-powerful father-in-law, had prevailed. Fifty yards of silk taffeta, in a hue somewhere between cream and ivory, chosen to match the Burano lace veil that had belonged to her grandmother Bouvier, had been needed to create the dress. The off-the-shoulder straps and bodice enhanced her slim physique, emphasizing her waist. The skirt, stiff and generously wide, was adorned with ruffled ribbons and a scattering of tiny orange blossoms handcrafted by the seamstresses of Ann Lowe, the celebrated African-American designer who created dreamy gowns for wealthy New York ladies and Hollywood divas. In fact, the beautiful dress Jackie wore that day was not the one she had been trying on for eight weeks at the atelier. Ten days before the wedding, a pipe had burst in the designer's shop, and the water had irreparably ruined the dress, which was almost finished. It would have been a tragedy for the shop's reputation, so Ann Lowe forced her seamstresses into secrecy, bought back the very costly fabric at her own expense, hired other trustworthy girls, and, working night and day, managed to deliver that fabulous dress by the agreed date. To entertain guests at the reception, the bride and groom hired the melodious voice of Meyer Davis, accompanied by his orchestra. During their first dance to the romantic song "I Married an Angel," played by the orchestra, the guests were able to admire the twirls of the bride in her flowing, hastily made gown.

The wedding ceremony at St. Mary's Church in Newport, September 12, 1953.

*Upon leaving the church, the bride and groom were greeted by a crowd
of 800 guests, who were joined by a further 400 people for the reception
held at Hammersmith Farm, the lavish estate of Jackie's stepfather.*

On her wrist, Jackie sported a precious diamond bracelet that her husband had given her the night before as a wedding gift, while in her hand she held a pink and white bouquet of orchids and gardenias. The finishing touch was a simple pearl necklace that would become one of her favorite pieces of jewelry for the rest of her life.

After the party, Jackie put on a delicate gray Chanel suit, hugged her mother and sister, and drove off with Jack beneath a cloud of rice and confetti, heading for the airport where a private flight would take them to New York. After spending their wedding night at the Waldorf Astoria, the couple left for a honeymoon in Acapulco, Mexico. Serving as a romantic backdrop to those happy days was a pink stone villa built atop a sandstone cliff, overlooking an enchanting bay. They went fishing and water-skiing and flipped through copies of the new issue of *Life* that portrayed them together once again, this time as husband and wife. What the press halfway around the world immediately called "the most glamorous couple of the century" had just been born.

The bride and groom pose together with bridesmaids and groomsmen during the reception. Pictured on the left is the cutting of the cake.

Above, Jackie and her husband open the dance floor to the love song "I Married an Angel," played by the Meyer Davis Orchestra.

On the right, the bouquet toss, captured by photographer Brooks Kraft.

The Perfect Wife
(1952–1960)

Torn between her role as a mother and her husband's campaign, Jackie impressed upon the world her style of haute couture gowns and movie-star smiles. But behind that dazzling image was a marriage full of difficulties, fractured by JFK's betrayals.

With her elegance and cosmopolitan appeal, at age 24 Jackie embodied the idealized image of the young American bride. Her radiant face jumped out of the pages of women's magazines such as *McCall's* and *Life*, in which she was portrayed in a photoshoot celebrating her new life. In the space of five days, more than a thousand pictures were taken of her, intended to illustrate an article chronicling her daily life alongside Senator Kennedy. They were photographed together, at his office desk in the Senate, but also on the Georgetown University campus that Jackie had returned to in order to further her studies of American history. "The Senator's Wife Goes Back to School," the magazine had headlined. More pictures were taken in the privacy of their new apartment, the love nest she had always dreamed of. After spending a short time in Jack's parents' home, the couple had taken up residence in Washington, D.C., in the Georgetown neighborhood. While furnishing their first apartment, she had imagined a normal everyday life, alongside a husband who came home every night at five o'clock. The reality was very different. "Life with him was a race," Jackie recalled, thinking back to the early years of marriage. As soon as she became Mrs. Kennedy, she found herself caught in a whirlwind of events in the run-up to Jack's 1954 midterm elections.

The newlyweds in a photobooth snapshot taken while they were on their honeymoon in Acapulco in 1953.

After the wedding, Jackie returned to her studies. In these images, taken for Life magazine, she says goodbye to her husband as she leaves the house, then attends classes at Georgetown University.

After all, she loved his ambition and impulses and passionately supported her husband's dreams, which, at that moment, coincided perfectly with her own. Together they attended dinner parties with a few dozen select and influential guests, as well as the social events that formed the beating heart of the capital's political life. More than anything else, Jackie longed to be the perfect wife to her husband. From the beginning she did everything she could to personify this dazzling self-image and make herself irresistible in his eyes, even learning to cook (with mediocre results), playing bridge (loved by him and loathed by her), and taking golf lessons. Around the same time, the young bride began to sense that that marriage would be anything but a fairy tale, as she was confronted with two issues she had not anticipated. The first concerned her husband's health.

Immediately after their marriage, the Kennedys lived in Georgetown, moving four times to different houses.

Above, in the living room of their apartment, they choose pictures for their wedding album.

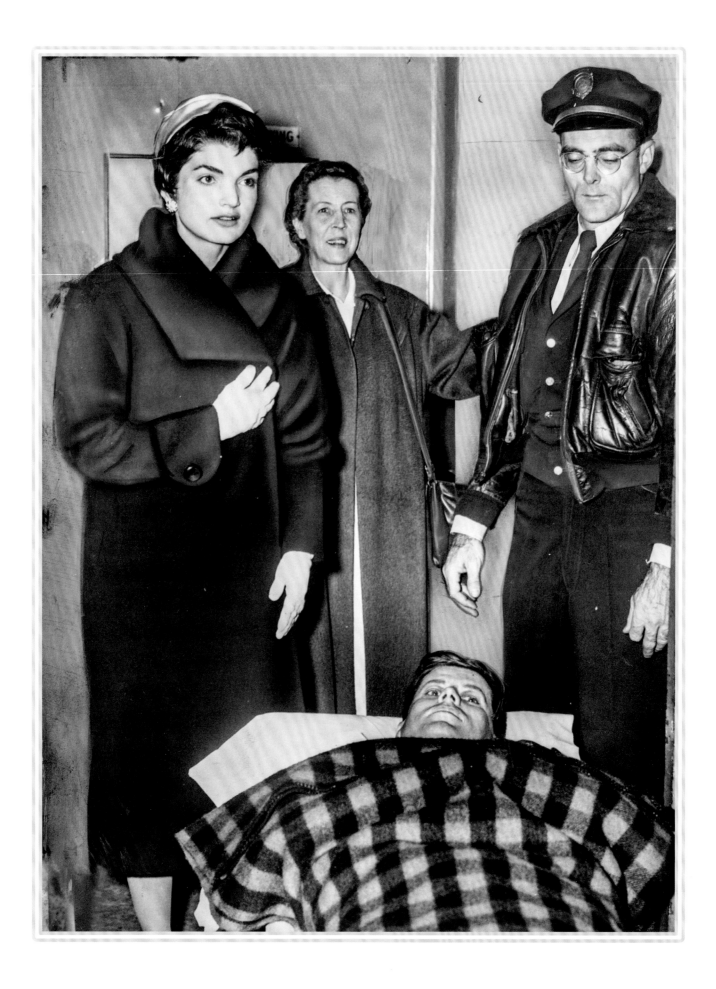

Jack had made physical vigor and youth his selling points, being photographed throwing a baseball to his brothers or posing athletically in front of his desk in the Senate. In reality, since childhood he had suffered from excruciating back pain that forced him to spend long periods of time in bed, during which he devoted himself passionately to reading. The legends of King Arthur and the Knights of the Round Table lived by his bedside, and, as he grew older, he became fond of the writings of Winston Churchill. Jack had written in 1940, in only six months, *Why England Slept*, an essay inspired by a Winston Churchill's book on the events that had led the United Kingdom to World War II that became an instant best seller.

On public occasions Jack always appeared at his best, striving to hide the pains that plagued him behind a smile and downplaying his medical misadventures as much as possible when he was obliged to talk about them. No one but family and his inner circle of friends was aware of the true state of his health. By the time he returned from his honeymoon, his condition had deteriorated. He could no longer climb the stairs or walk the long corridors of the Senate and tried to hide from everyone the crutches he was now using more and more often. The excruciating pains had convinced him to consider undergoing complicated spine surgery that posed serious risks, exacerbated by Addison's disease, the autoimmune disorder he had recently been diagnosed with. "I would rather die than spend the rest of my life on crutches," he confessed to his wife when he decided to have the surgery. Three days after the procedure, he developed an infection that kept him on the verge of death for weeks. He asked for Jackie, but doctors forbade anyone to enter his room.

She knew she was in danger of losing him and vowed that she would never again allow anyone to keep her away from Jack in his time of need. A promise she would honor when fate again imposed this decisive test on her, with a far more tragic outcome. Jack survived the surgery and she became a constant, encouraging presence during his long convalescence in the hospital.

Jackie assists her husband after back surgery that nearly cost him his life. Above, one of the rare images of Kennedy on crutches during his recovery.

Kennedy and his wife Jackie on the Capitol steps in Washington in 1954, photographed on their first public outing after his back surgery.

During those months, they were working together on the book Profiles in Courage, *for which Kennedy would win the Pulitzer Prize.*

She devoted every moment to him, patiently caring for him and then, as he began to feel better, taking notes, reading to him from newspapers and poems, writing letters to politicians for him, and helping him do research for his new book, *Profiles in Courage,* for which Kennedy would win the Pulitzer Prize. Seven months later, Jack had recovered his resolve, but not his health. He flaunted his irresistible smile and perfect tan to the press as he climbed the Capitol steps, but was in fact forced to wear a back brace and hide the pain behind an unimpeachable mask, relying heavily on painkillers.

After the difficult months at her husband's bedside, Jackie took a long vacation with her sister Lee to the French Riviera, where Jack joined her after stopping in Sweden to spend a few days with his new mistress. She was but the latest in an endless series of women who had always punctuated Kennedy's tumultuous love life.

This was the other aspect of the marriage that Jackie had underestimated: her husband's inexhaustible inclination to infidelity. He was in love, yet he continued to behave as he had as a bachelor, when all he had to do was snap his fingers to get any girl he wanted. He had the charm of a Hollywood actor, and women literally fell at his feet. It seems that he had begun cheating on Jackie as early as their honeymoon, and then continued to disappear from the receptions they attended together in Washington. His wife was well aware that he often ended his evenings at the Mayflower Hotel, making his way to the eighth-floor suite where a new and uninhibited girl awaited him. Jackie remained silent out of love, continuing to appear flawless at his side in public, serene and reassuring, smiling at photographers as she posed on his arm in her evening gown.

Those shots would help build a public image of the Kennedys that was in complete conflict with their reality. Jackie learned early on how to conduct a marriage constantly on a knife's edge, bearing Jack's betrayals with an elegance that was entirely her own. Most of all, she learned to wait up for him late into the night, never asking him uncomfortable questions. Whenever he came home, she greeted him with her charming, enigmatic smile.

After three years of marriage, Jack's hectic schedule was in full swing, forcing him to jump through hoops to manage his political and marital commitments. He would make speeches all over the country, staying away from home for days at a time. Jackie's loneliness was sweetened by the discovery that she was finally pregnant, just as she moved with Jack to a cottage in the country, on a hill overlooking the Potomac River. It would be an idyllic place in which to raise children, so she began setting up a nursery for the baby, equipping it with everything she needed. But plans to expand the family met with an unhappy fate. She gave birth to a baby girl, Arabella, who did not survive the delivery. It was a heartbreaking bereavement that she had to face alone: Jack was once again far away, traveling through Europe and unreachable by phone, as he was aboard a yacht, probably in the company of some girl. It was Bobby, Jack's younger brother, who took care of his sister-in-law, arranging the little one's funeral and consoling Jackie while waiting for the return of her husband, who did not come home until five days later. A year on, Jackie was expecting again, just as she rushed to New York to pay her last respects to her father, who had passed away at the age of sixty-six from cancer. Along with relatives and a few friends, the funeral was attended by a host of veiled women who settled in the last pew of the church, completely unknown to the family. They were Black Jack's mistresses, who had come to bid him a final farewell.

The couple on vacation in a photo from the 1950s.

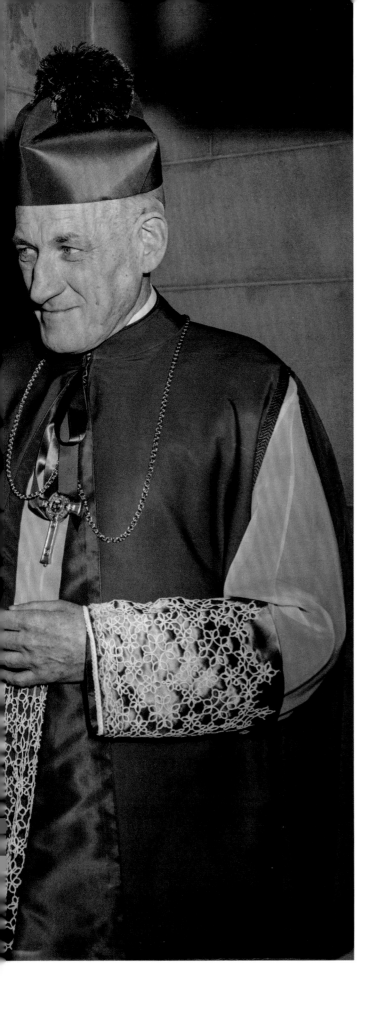

Three months later, on November 27, 1957, Jackie gave birth to Caroline. It was Jack who placed her in her mother's arms, as attentive and caring as ever. A few weeks later, the couple appeared on the cover of *Life* with their baby. Jackie was radiant; she had finally achieved everything she desired. Fulfilled by motherhood, Jackie's personality was evolving along with her style. She had always had a weakness for haute couture dresses and all things French, so she filled her wardrobe with elegant clothing that reflected her taste and culture. Her image was no longer that of a simple American girl, but of a sophisticated woman with a European allure.

Jackie holds baby Caroline Bouvier Kennedy during her baptism at St. Patrick's Cathedral in New York City.

"I have learned that there is a big difference between what people think and what I know to be true."

A snapshot with daughter Caroline taken during a break from an official press photoshoot in Hyannis Port, in the summer of 1958.

In this intimate and cheerful photo, Jackie smiles at her daughter Caroline shortly after her third birthday party in the summer of 1960.

These images, taken months in advance, were used on Christmas cards sent out with holiday greetings.

The change posed only one dilemma to the Kennedys' political entourage: how would the American voting public react? By the summer of 1958, for the first time, JFK had made his voice heard as a United States presidential candidate, ushering in one of the most legendary election campaigns in history. The possibility of playing Jackie's politics card in view of future elections was a highly controversial topic. Her sophisticated elegance, so different from that of the demure First Ladies of the past, could prove to be either a triumph or a disaster. She was put to the test during the summer recess of the Senate proceedings, when the Kennedys had the opportunity to meet Churchill aboard a vessel destined to play a pivotal role in Jackie's life. The meeting took place on the *Christina,* the yacht owned by Greek shipowner Aristotle Onassis. The former wartime frigate had been converted into a luxury yacht on which celebrities like Greta Garbo and entrepreneurs like Gianni Agnelli were invited. Wearing a Saint Laurent Trapeze dress, Jackie stepped aboard for the first time on the arm of her husband, who was more excited than she was to come face to face with one of his political heroes, who inspired him to fine-tune his campaign.

Mother and daughter paint together during a vacation in Hyannis Port.

"We should all do something
to right the wrongs that
we see and not just
complain about them."

Jackie gives a TV interview to support Kennedy's campaign.

Upon returning to the United States, JFK's Senate seat was reconfirmed with 73 percent of the vote, the highest popular margin a candidate had ever achieved in Massachusetts. He was ready to attempt the 1960 presidential race. Beginning in January, Jackie joined her husband on the campaign trail. She appeared at his side wrapped in a red Givenchy coat, with a copy of the book *War and Peace* under her arm, winning everyone over with her soft voice and apparent shyness. Kennedy's detractors judged her aloof and arrogant, but each of her appearances drew in crowds, attracting far more attention than her husband. Educated and multilingual, always elegant and smiling, she soon proved to be a winning card. She conversed in French at Cajun festivals in Louisiana and in Spanish with Puerto Ricans in New York. Her mastery of Italian turned her into a star during the Columbus Day parade, when she walked the streets alongside her husband, surrounded by crowds on both sides.

After the convention that officially confirmed Kennedy as the Democratic presidential candidate, media pressure became increasingly intense for Jackie. While many encouraged the senator to appear more often with his beautiful wife by his side, magazines such as *Women's Wear Daily* targeted the fancy and costly sense of style and the extravagant expenses she incurred on couture outfits. To reporters who accused her of spending thirty thousand dollars a year on Balenciaga and Givenchy dresses, she replied "I couldn't spend that much unless I wore sable underwear." Ever flawless, she let her innate sense of style guide her, even when it came simply to choosing the shade of a boiled wool suit or the height of her kitten heels, low-heeled pumps from 3.5 cm to 4.5 cm high at the most, decidedly sophisticated and bon ton.

Senator Kennedy and Jackie in New Hampshire, surrounded by supporters in the Presidential Primary.

The Boston Globe

MORNING
EDITION

JACK, IN WALK

Uproar for Adlai
Delays Balloting

Galleries Wild Over Stevenson;
2 Favorite Sons Quit for Kennedy

EXTRA

Die Is Cast, So Kennedy
Takes Nap in His Hideout

Speed Urged on
Security Council

Plea for Red China
Hinted by New York

Be Sure
Red China
Plane Probe

Belgian Commandos Seize
Congo Capital City, Airport

Two DC Airliners Down
With 89; Two Missing

Flash Storms
Raise Havoc in
Boston Area

6 Lively Kids in Kennedy Box
Act Like They're at the Circus

Red China May Grab
Foothold in Africa

U.S. ROYAL SALE
AT BETTER QUALITY TIRES

A new haircut, shorter and more voluminous, enhanced the unique shape of her face. That legendary hairstyle, destined to be copied by millions of women, was created for her by Kenneth Battelle, the hairdresser who would become her stylist of choice. At the time, she was still an unknown young American lady, and he was in his early career, working at Helena Rubinstein's beauty salon on Fifth Avenue. When Battelle opened his salon in Manhattan, Marilyn Monroe also became one of his devoted clients. Jackie had many things in common with the actress, besides a hairdresser and her husband's attention. Her low, whispery, vaguely childlike voice was reminiscent of her rival's.

Jackie always played a key role in her husband's political career. Attentive and present, she read with Kennedy the press reactions to the announcement of his candidacy in 1960.

The campaign also greatly involved Jackie,
pictured here with Kennedy during
a meeting with the press.

Together with her radiant, natural makeup, Jackie's look during that era was complemented with a splash of what would become her favorite perfume. It was considered the most expensive in the world, with a mix of floral notes: Bulgarian rose, ylang-ylang and an explosion of tuberose as top notes, jasmine and may rose as heart notes, and a warm base of musk and sandalwood. Such is the olfactory pyramid of Joy, Jean Patou's fragrance created in 1929. That scent hinted at her innate class, reflected also in a style that Jackie, along with Audrey Hepburn, embodied: the elegance of the 1960s. The two women also resembled each other in their androgynous physiques, achieved thanks to strict diet and a lot of sports, but also by indulging in cigarettes. Jackie had smoked since her college years to avoid putting on weight, although she was almost never caught with a cigarette in her hand in front of photographers. In those days, they were constantly lurking in anticipation of her public appearances, along with the swarm of reporters who followed Kennedy's every move.

The Kennedys bid farewell to little Caroline before departing for Philadelphia ahead of the 1960 election campaign. Jackie was expecting John Jr.'s birth.

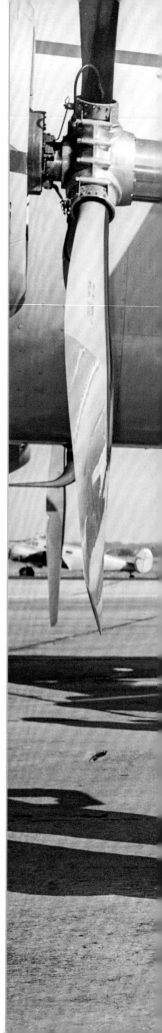

Jackie knew this would be the price of climbing the political ladder, but she resented the intrusion into the privacy of her marriage. She was annoyed by gossip about her husband's escapades, disliked answering any kind of personal question, and raged at every snub hurled at her by newspapers and political opponents, while Jack remained impassive, eyeing people coolly as if they were pawns on a chessboard. Jackie's problem was that she often saw herself as one of them. She detested the noisy, crowded parties she was obliged to attend to meet congressmen and senators. Those men reminded her of crude jackals always looking for votes, and their wives bored her with their predictable and monotonous conversations. Jackie was more cultured, refined, and intelligent than most of them. She had studied at the best schools and had spent a long time in Europe. She had flair, taste, and imagination. These were the gifts of a First Lady, and it would not be long before she began demonstrating them.

Jackie and her husband photographed working side by side in the senator's Washington office.

"It is time for a new
generation of leadership,
to cope with new problems
and new opportunities.
For there is a new world
to be won."

(John Fitzgerald Kennedy)

Pictured during a rally in New York City in October 1960.

The couple parades in a convertible amid supporters in New York.

America's Queen (1960–1963)

During their thousand days in the White House, the Kennedys transformed that political landmark into the Kingdom of Camelot. With her radiant beauty, the First Lady won everyone over. And thanks to her, the rest of the world would discover a new, young, cosmopolitan, and refined America.

"Ask not what your country can do for you: ask what you can do for your country." With these words, spoken in front of the Capitol, John Fitzgerald Kennedy introduced himself as the new political leader of the United States. At forty-three, he was the first Catholic president, the first born in the twentieth century, and the first of the television era. Jackie shone like a star by his side. From that moment, she was no longer just Kennedy's wife, but one of the youngest First Ladies in history. She was about to turn thirty-one, and, along with this victory, would soon celebrate the arrival of Jack's long-awaited male heir. "My wife and I look forward to the birth of this new administration, and of a new baby," JFK announced soon after the proclamation. On November 25, 1960, exactly seventeen days after his famous father's election, John Jr. was born by Cesarean section. He had needed to be incubated and remained with his mother in the hospital for several weeks. Jackie recovered just in time to attend the inauguration ceremony, an event destined to go down in history. All the eyes of the world were on Washington when it was announced from the stage: "Ladies and gentlemen, the President of the United States and the First Lady," as Jacqueline appeared on Jack's arm, her gracious smile framed by aristocratic cheekbones.

The family smiles as little John Jr. is carried through the White House door.

She wore an ice-colored sleeveless gown with a sheer silk chiffon top, embellished with a bodice embroidered with silver silk thread and beads. It was created by Bergdorf Goodman's tailor shop in New York, based on sketches and suggestions provided by Jackie. Because of her decided taste, she personally chose every detail of the looks she wore during her first appearances as First Lady. The night before the inauguration, she looked regal in a floor-length, trapeze silk gown at the gala hosted at the National Guard Armory by Frank Sinatra with Hollywood stars and musical greats from Gene Kelly to Nat King Cole, Tony Curtis to Ella Fitzgerald.

RIGHT: On January 20, 1961, Jackie make her first official appearance as First Lady on stage with her husband and Vice President Lyndon Johnson, with his wife. On the right, Kennedy's parents can be seen.

LEFT: The presidential couple leave their George-town home for their first official visit to the White House on Inauguration Day.

The next morning, she selected a pale-colored coat with large buttons and fur collar and muff. The *coup de théâtre* was a cloth pillbox hat that no one would ever wear in the cold Washington winter. It stood out like a beacon in an indistinct tide of mink headgear: "a gorgeous petal in a dowdy bouquet of fur," as it was called by the press. Thanks to a pair of dresses, a coat, and a cape, she became the world's most elegant First Lady within just two days. And she would soon become both an American and an international fashion icon. Published on the front pages of newspapers around the world, her clothes were more than simply personal whim or glimmers of emotion: they were a fashion statement from the wife of the President of the United States of America. "I'm getting good at it, now that fashion is more important than politics and the press pays more attention to Jackie's clothes than to my speeches." With this line, JFK voiced the change in the pace of public attention that underscored Jackie's every appearance. Nothing was left to chance when it came to her outfits, designed to convey charisma and a sense of innovation, but equally tradition and an attachment to values. At a time when women wore wide skirts with cinched waists and puffed sleeves, Jackie favored the clean lines of Chanel and the slim silhouette of Givenchy and Balenciaga. But after becoming First Lady of the United States, she could no longer flaunt her beloved French luxury brands—to do so would have been considered an unpatriotic faux pas. So she promised her husband that from then on she would wear only American haute couture.

Oleg Cassini was the designer who dressed Jackie during the three years of the Kennedy presidency. Here he is photographed at the Pierre Hotel during a press presentation of his creations for the first official looks worn by the First Lady.

On the right is a sketch of the coat Jackie wore on Inauguration Day, with a fur collar and a matching hat.

What she needed was a new signature designer. The role would be awarded to the simple elegance of Oleg Cassini, the designer who had imported the style of the great European *maisons* to the United States. Born in Paris to a noble Italian-Russian family, he had not yet established himself, but had already worked with (and got engaged to) the divine Grace Kelly. During the years of the Kennedy presidency, he made more than three hundred outfits for Jackie, bringing to the world a style that established his success. His boiled wool suits, boat necklines, trapeze dresses, cuff dress embellished with a high collar, gala ball gowns, and imperial style became indelible elements of Cassini's new signature fashion. Thanks to him, Jackie learned to dress with an ultimate synthesis of just a few pieces and one standout item. It could be a hat, a piece of jewelry, or a bright color, such as orange, pink, or lime green. Wearing those vivid tones, she stood out like a flower in official photos,

the only spot of color in a sea of gray clothes. Her wardrobe alternated between day and evening styles, overcoats, and numerous skirts, high-waisted pants, and sleeveless sheath dresses. She favored knee-length flared cuts and egg-shaped silhouette coats with large buttons. Over evening gowns she often wore a long cape with a simple cut instead of an overcoat. Cassini orchestrated her wardrobe as if it were a concert. Each look was complemented by matching gloves, shoes, and handbags. The finishing touch was the ever-present pillbox hat, a tambourine-shaped hat that matched the rest of her wardrobe and was destined to write a key chapter in the history of women's fashion. A symbol of the allure expected of a First Lady, it was inspired by a flat, brimless model that originated in the 1930s and was revived and made famous by Roy Halston, then an up-and-coming New York designer who was destined to become the leading designer of disco fashion in the 1970s.

Detatchable sable collar
Beige Wool

"It is really frightening to lose your anonymity at 31. I feel as though I have just turned into a piece of public property."

Jackie in an official portrait at the White House.

Adding the finishing touches to Jackie's style was the jewelry: earrings, rings, bracelets, and necklaces made by the best-known jewelers, which she turned into emblems of a new and modern style. This is exactly what she did with one of her favorites: the Berry Sprig Brooch that her husband had made for the birth of their son, giving it to her that year for Christmas. Even though he was working on organizing the new presidential administration, Jack had found time to go in person to Tiffany's in New York and oversee the design. Created by renowned jewelry designer Jean Schlumberger, the berry brooch was designed to represent and celebrate both of the couple's children. Made of yellow gold with 37 diamonds and 80 rubies, it consisted of a slightly larger berry, with more conspicuous stones, representing Caroline, Jackie's daughter, and a smaller berry celebrating John Jr. It was a precious and elegant piece of designer jewelry that Jackie fell in love with at first sight, both for its sculptural lines and its great sentimental value. She chose to wear it on her first official trip abroad as First Lady to Canada in May 1961, when the press was abuzz with talk of her suit in the same shade of red as the Royal Canadian Mounted Police uniform.

It was the beginning of a style upheld throughout the entire presidential term. What until then had been considered flaws, such as unconventional beauty, un-American elegance, and a predilection for French fashion and cuisine, all of a sudden became assets. Jackie's charisma became more apparent than ever during the presidential visit to France. The motorcade in which the Kennedys were traveling was greeted with shouts of "Vive Jacqueline!" along the entire ten-mile route between the airport and downtown Paris.

Looking impeccable in an Oleg Cassini suit and pearls on an official visit to Paris in June 1961, surrounded by crowds.

Only the Beatles would receive a similarly triumphant reception. It was clear that it was not the President but his wife who was attracting the crowds. According to President Charles de Gaulle, the influx of more than a million people was owed to Mrs. Kennedy's charming of the French people. And of him as well. During the luncheon held at the Élysée Palace, Jackie entertained him by demonstrating her mastery of the French language and history. They talked at length about Louis XVI and the intricate genealogy of the

Wearing an evening dress, Jackie heads to a reception in Paris during the Kennedys' official visit to France.
Pictured on the right with French President Charles de Gaulle at a reception in the Hall of Mirrors at the Palace of Versailles, held on the evening of June 2, 1961.

last Bourbons. Then de Gaulle, leaning over the table, told Jack, "Your wife knows the history of France far better than any French woman." The next day, Jackie visited Paris, to which she had not returned since her last trip as a student. She went back to admire Manet's Olympia, one of her favorite paintings, and visited the Château de Malmaison, whose imperial-style furnishings fascinated her greatly. She then allowed herself an hour of freedom, touring the city alone, under the discreet vigilance of a security agent, at dusk.

Much of the luggage that the Kennedys had brought to Paris consisted of Jackie's wardrobe. For such an occasion she had added some pieces from French fashion houses to her American wardrobe. At Versailles, during the official reception dinner in the dazzling Hall of Mirrors, she appeared wearing a pearl-embroidered white satin dress with a long silk cape signed by Givenchy, in homage to French haute couture. In her hair she wore diamond clips that shimmered under the glow of the evocative candlelight. The next day, French newspapers enthusiastically reported on the evening, paying tribute to Jackie with headlines such as "Apotheosis at Versailles" and "Paris Has a Queen." Aware of that wave of popularity, during the pre-departure press conference President Kennedy won everyone over with his irony. "I do not think it altogether inappropriate to introduce myself to this audience," he declared. "I am the man who accompanied Jacqueline Kennedy to Paris."

The next stop was Vienna, where a summit with embattled Russian Prime Minister Nikita Khrushchev awaited them. These were the years of the Cold War, and the discussions were disastrous. Tempers cooled only during the concluding dinner. Once again, the eyes of those present were on Jackie, wrapped in a pink Cassini gown that enchanted everyone, including the Soviet leader. "First Lady Conquers Even Khrushchev," headlined the New York *Times*. "Smitten Khrushchev Is Jackie's Happy Escort," the New York *Herald-Tribune* echoed.

Before leaving Europe, they made one last stop in London to attend the christening of Jackie's niece, daughter of her sister Lee and her second husband, Prince Stanislav Radziwill. That evening, all four of them had been invited to dinner at Buckingham Palace, guests of Elizabeth II. The queen wore the famous Cobalt Dress, a blue tulle gown, chosen with great care so as not to risk being outshone by the now-legendary elegance of the American First Lady. The British press once again reported enthusiasm for her style, and *Time* magazine crowned Jackie "The First Lady of Fashion."

Above, Jackie Kennedy converses with Russian Prime Minister Nikita Khrushchev in Vienna.

On the opposite page, she poses for an official portrait at Buckingham Palace with Queen Elizabeth II and Prince Philip during the Kennedys' 1961 visit to the United Kingdom.

Among the Kennedys' most lavish receptions at the White House was the one held on May 11, 1962 in honor of French Minister of Culture André Malraux, pictured here next to Jackie.

On the opposite page, Jackie beams in the pink Christian Dior gown she wore that evening, next to her husband and the guest of honor with his wife.

That triumphant reception abroad, completely unexpected, greatly boosted her self-confidence. Upon her return to the United States, she felt that she had won her husband's trust and was newly confident in her abilities. She was no longer a young wife in the shadow of a powerful man, but a prominent international figure. The results were quick to follow. From then on, the spotlight would be on her in a continuous media siege. Jackie became one of the most important presidential public-relations resources and, thanks to her, Washington soon became the American capital of culture and taste. The new lifestyle of the White House included an intense social life, punctuated by official invitations and concerts, performances, and ballets, to which Nobel Prize winners, writers, poets, and filmmakers were invited. These were lavish receptions, unimaginable during the presidencies of Eisenhower or Truman. When it came to state dinners, the Kennedys hosted legendary soirées, such as the one held on May 11, 1962, in honor of the French Minister of Culture, André Malraux. Jackie spent weeks compiling the guest list, a list of celebrities that included playwright Tennessee Williams, novelist Saul Bellow, director Elia Kazan, painter Mark Rothko, ballet dancer George Balanchine, and conductor Leonard Bernstein. A week later, a fundraiser was held to celebrate the President's 44th birthday at Madison Square Garden. It was an event that celebrated Jack, instead of Jackie, in front of 15,000 people, and the star of the evening was the ravishing Marilyn Monroe. She suddenly appeared beneath a spotlight singing *Happy Birthday, Mr. President,* swathed in a dazzling see-through gown. Three months later, on August 5, Marilyn would be found dead, tantalizing the pens of journalists and prompting all kinds of speculation about the cause of her suicide. With an icy demeanor, Jackie would simply say "She will be remembered forever."

"She seduced you with a smile, changed your life and you didn't even know why."

(Truman Capote)

Pictured in evening attire during a dinner for the America's Cup Race.

During the years of her husband's presidency, Jackie attended countless ceremonies.
Above, she attends the launching of the nuclear submarine Lafayette.

On the opposite page, she boards a plane to Florida.

"No one else looked like her, spoke like her, wrote like her, or was so original in the way she did things."

(Edward Kennedy)

Always smiling and wearing the ever-present pillbox hat created by Roy Halston that Jackie turned into a classic symbol of feminine elegance.

Above, Jackie Kennedy distributes gifts and talks with young residents of the National Institute for the Protection of Children during an official visit to Mexico City in June 1962.

On the right, she is pictured leaving Mass in Middleburg, Virginia.

127

She knew that for her husband, women were just fiercely passionate encounters destined to come to a swift end. That is why she turned a blind eye to his affairs, especially when they were in public. While she was dancing the twist with Secretary of Defense Robert McNamara in a crowded room, Jack was romancing in his study with one of his many mistresses. In private, however, things were different. One day she threw open the door to the study where Jack was busy working and stood before him, pointing her index finger in his face, from which finger dangled a pair of lace panties found under a White House couch. "You find out who they belong to; they're not my size," she told him, throwing them on the floor and leaving the room, her back straight and her head held high. The owner of said panties was a young secretary with blond hair and milky skin, just the way Jack liked them. Yet despite her husband's constant distractions, Jackie was the one the public kept the spotlight on, always ready to catch her in the act and accuse her of imaginary infidelities. It was rumored that she had settled scores with her husband by indulging in celebrity affairs with the likes of Frank Sinatra and William Holden. The rumors became more persistent when Jackie was a guest of Gianni Agnelli on his yacht with a group of friends. They were cleverly photographed by the paparazzi, framing them as being alone and providing the tabloids with evidence to fuel gossip about a liaison between the First Lady and the Italian businessman. No one in Washington believed such inferences. In fact, what really bothered the White House was that the First Lady's social gatherings threatened to alienate the Kennedys from voters. The vacuous debate sparked by Jackie's vacations came to an abrupt halt shortly thereafter, when far more serious issues loomed on the horizon that tested the nation and strengthened the presidential couple. Jackie and her husband were never closer to each other than during the terrible autumn of the Cuban Missile Crisis, when a miscalculation on Washington's part could have unleashed nuclear hell. The Secret Service had advised Jackie to leave the White House with her children, to get closer to the bomb shelter. She had refused. During the days and nights of the missile crisis, she and Jack walked together in silence, sharing without speaking the same anguish and breathing a sigh of relief together when it was announced that Khrushchev had given orders to dismantle the missiles. It was one of the few public moments in which they held each other in a long embrace. To commemorate those days of shared suffering, he gave her a silver Tiffany paperweight calendar with the fateful thirteen days highlighted. It would remain on her writing desk forever.

Jackie on vacation in Italy, drinking coffee in Ravello with Gianni Agnelli and Prince Radziwill, husband of her sister Lee.

During those weeks, the influence of the political sphere over the private sphere had become overwhelming, and Jackie began to fear that presidential life would disrupt the children's routines. Yet, on the contrary, her years in the White House proved to be the most intimate for the family. This is testified to by pictures depicting the family at Christmas, amid gifts and decorations, revealing an intimately playful side that could not be shown through official channels. Also confirming this impression are Jackie's personal recollections, such as that of a particularly merry Halloween, during which she improvised costumes to hide their identities while they accompanied the children trick-or-treating. They passed by several houses incognito, until someone noticed the Secret Service and their cover was blown, forcing them to return to the White House.

When she was not busy with official engagements, Jackie's daily life in the White House was devoted to her children. Above, she plays with baby John Jr. in the nursery created especially for him.

On the opposite page, she reads a fairy tale to Caroline.

Jackie with her daughter Caroline, assisting a class in the kindergarten set up in the White House by her own initiative.

The first time she had visited what would become her new home, she had been disappointed: "I felt like a moth banging against the glass. The windows hadn't been opened in years," she recalled. She decided that that residence would become an oasis of serenity, especially for the children. So she dove into the project of transforming the presidential home into a warm and welcoming haven, brimming with art and books. She also sensed that the symbol of national unity sought in 1791 by George Washington no longer reflected American history. Over time, the house had undergone countless transformations, as it had been redecorated with the succession of each new president, eventually losing its original appearance. So Jackie began the grand restyling project that would restore Washington to its former glory: the American capital would have its own Versailles. She had furniture, paintings, and works of art that had once graced the state rooms put back on display. Wearing a white shirt, jogging pants, and flat-heeled riding boots, she rummaged through the storage spaces for hours and had everything she found not to her taste removed from the rooms. She got forgotten historical pieces found in cellars and attics restored, then contrasted them with modern furnishings in a new sense of style that was completely unfamiliar to America in those years. The next step was to establish a Fine Arts Committee that would oversee the work, involving historians, museum curators, and antiquarians who, in turn, persuaded dozens of collectors to donate period works and furnishings originating from the White House but that had ended up on the market over the centuries. She became personally involved in asking for loans and donations to find the original furnishings and, when that was not possible, to procure identical pieces of furniture from the same historical periods.

The results of that grand makeover were shown to the public in a legendary documentary broadcast on nationwide television. It was an unprecedented success that won an Emmy and went straight to the hearts of Americans.

The presidential couple in front of the White House in Washington.

On February 14, 1962, Jackie personally greeted sixty million television viewers who watched enraptured as she showed off the new look of the presidential residence. Wearing a red dress cut just below the knee and low-heeled shoes, Jackie walked around the rooms, illustrating every detail. Her charm was already well known, but many were also surprised to discover the First Lady's nonchalant expertise as she listed the names of painters, furniture makers, and decorators as a true connoisseur of antiques. Far from being an iconoclast, as many had feared, Jackie proved herself to be a champion of historical conservation and restoration. Most intriguing to viewers was a visit to the second floor, to the private apartments where the First Family lived. Jackie had transformed the Prince of Wales suite into a private kitchen with an adjoining dining room for the sole use of the President and his family, decorating it with wallpaper depicting scenes from the American Revolution.

Behind the scenes of A Tour of the White House with Mrs. John F. Kennedy *with journalist Charles Collingwood.*

Since the presidential residence was now to accommodate a young couple with two children, she had arranged for a large play area in the grounds with swings and a treehouse, as well as new rooms for the children. Caroline, who was five years old at the time, was already a horse lover, so Jackie decided to decorate her equestrian-themed room with country paintings and, of course, a rocking horse, while a proper nursery was created for newborn John Jr. The master bedroom in the White House was officially the Lincoln Room, but President Kennedy had his own room where he slept when work forced him to keep late hours. Jackie decorated it according to her husband's preferences, making it as practical and comfortable as possible. She also had a room of her own. A majestic hallway led to her private bedroom, which remained an intimate and secluded place. She replaced the heavy green drapes with lighter, thinner curtains that let in light and turned the window into a focal point of the room. Most First Ladies had used the space adjacent to the master bedroom as a wardrobe, but Jackie transformed it into a sitting room. She preferred to keep her immense wardrobe in a room near the bathroom and her private bedroom. Chinese porcelain, drapes with a daisy pattern, and closets hidden in the paneling graced Jackie's private sanctuary. She also redecorated the Glen Ora house, the rented country home in Virginia where the couple spent weekends, with the same taste. And even Air Force One, the presidential plane that could be turned into a cozy alcove when needed and into which Marilyn had also climbed several times, bundled up to disguise her renowned curves and wearing a black wig over her platinum hair.

Caroline and John Jr. in the White House gardens, set up for them with swings and children's toys, in the spring of 1963. Behind them is Nanny Maude Shaw.

At that time, however, the most photographed woman in the world was not the Hollywood actress, but Jackie. Her compelling rise to fame seemed never-ending. After conquering the United States and France, she was on her way to making the rest of the world fall at her feet. A sea of pink, fuchsia, and turquoise saris greeted Jackie and her sister Lee during their unofficial three-week trip to India in March 1962. They were greeted in New Delhi by a cheering crowd that immediately dubbed the first lady "Ameriki Rani," or Queen of America. The Bouvier sisters mounted a regal elephant and camels, pursued throughout their stay by a flock of reporters and photographers. The countless articles that appeared in the press revealed details of the outfits designed for the occasion, from brightly hued sleeveless summer dresses to more formal gowns worn at gala dinners. They were designed by Oleg Cassini and another of the American designers Jackie had launched, Gustave Tassell. Among them all, the superb Peach Satin Dress, a knee-length silk gown in a particular shade of pink, chosen to pay homage to the exoticism of India and its colors, remained memorable. From that triumphant tour, the strained relations between the United States and India emerged strengthened, thanks in part to the understanding Jackie established with Prime Minister Jawaharlal Nehru, who was captivated by the charms of the woman so far from the mold of the previous First Ladies.

Greeted like a queen, Jackie landed in India in March 1962, welcomed by Prime Minister Jawaharlal Nehru.

On the right, an image taken at the residence of the Indian Prime Minister, posing next to Jackie along with his daughter Indira Gandhi and the U.S. Ambassador and his wife.

Jackie and sister Lee riding an elephant in Pakistan in 1962.

On the opposite page, Jackie's arrival in Jaipur, Rajasthan.

On the left page, Jackie disembarks at Amalfi Harbor in August 1962.

On this page, she loads a camera with film aboard the yacht of Gianni Agnelli, at the helm, and his wife Marella, on the left in a striped shirt.

The solid complicity established between the Bouvier sisters during the trip was strengthened when they found themselves a few months later in Amalfi, on the southern Italian coast. Lee had rented for them a splendid mansion overlooking the sea, nestled among lemon and orange blossoms. Villa Episcopio had a breathtaking view of the vast blue expanse of the Mediterranean, framed by the cliffs of Capri. Smiling and tanned and in tip-top shape, they strolled through the streets of the island and then plunged into the turquoise waters in the company of the jet-set stars who regularly frequented Italy. They were guests of the Agnellis on their yacht *Agneta* and danced late into the night in clubs to the tune of *Volare*.

It was a lighthearted, schedule-free vacation that made Jackie immensely happy and bound her forever to that stretch of Italian coastline, so much so that before she left she was made an honorary citizen of Ravello. In the village, shopkeepers called her "Jacchelì," and the beach at Conca dei Marini, where she went down every day to bathe, was renamed Jacqueline Kennedy Beach. During that memorable vacation, her iconic summer look was also born, consisting of leather sandals hand-sewn by local artisans, of which she owned an entire collection, paired with ankle-length white cigarette pants and huge sunglasses. Over her hair she knotted a Hermès scarf. Images of Jackie strolling around Capri went global. Won over by her grace, the whole world fell in love with her.

Pictured above on vacation in Italy, Jackie and Caroline pose under a sign welcoming them to the Amalfi Coast.

On the right, the First Lady becomes an honorary citizen of Ravello.

Relaxed in Ravello, Jackie draws while her sister Lee and husband Stanislas Radziwill play cards.

The Shattered Dream (1963–1968)

November 22, 1963 was a dark day in Dallas that brought a brutal end to an era. Eight unforgettable seconds shocked the world and broke Jackie's heart, forever making the Kennedy name legendary.

An entire generation would have an exact answer to the question, "Where were you when JFK was shot?" Anyone who lived through that tragic event remembers precisely the details of the eight seconds that changed history. Yet the fateful year of 1963, the Kennedys' *annus horribilis,* had begun under the best of circumstances, and nothing foreshadowed the tragedies that would seal Jackie's fate. Earlier in the year she had discovered that she was expecting a baby and had withdrawn almost entirely from public life. Despite the rest, baby Patrick was born severely prematurely. Wearing a surgical gown, Jack spent the night in the hospital next to his wife as the baby struggled to survive in a hyperbaric chamber. Seven years earlier, he had been away when their first daughter had died, while this time he was there to comfort his wife when news arrived that the baby had not made it. Jackie fell into a deep depression, eventually accepting an invitation from her sister, who suggested a cruise to the Mediterranean to banish sad thoughts. They had been invited aboard the yacht of Aristotle Onassis, a prominent Greek shipowner whom some tabloid newspapers referred to as Lee's lover. As soon as they boarded the *Christina,* a media storm broke out that exposed Jackie to her first real personal scandal.

On vacation in the Mediterranean, she visited museums and was enchanted by the classical statues. After Italy, she made stops in Greece and Morocco before returning to the United States.

Onassis had several pending legal disputes with the U.S. administration, was fresh from his divorce from his first wife, and was rumored to have been throwing wild parties since hosting the First Lady. The White House was flooded with letters of protest over what was considered a vacation aboard a playboy yacht by a mother who had just mourned the passing of baby Patrick. In reality, the two sisters spent most of the time alone, seeking solace from their grief. Onassis remained aloof, granting Jackie all the peace that his wealth and generosity could offer her. However, when photos began to circulate of them together while visiting archaeological sites in Istanbul and Izmir, Kennedy demanded that his wife return home. To American citizens, those pictures seemed disrespectful to the institutional duties of a First Lady, and she was well aware that she was creating problems for Jack with that behavior. "I was very sad after the death of my son and stayed away longer than was needed," she would later admit.

Leveraging her feelings of guilt, as soon as she returned to Washington Jack asked Jackie to accompany him to Texas, along with Vice President Lyndon Johnson and his wife, for an official visit. Jackie agreed without hesitation, conscious of her duties. That trip would be an important test of the President's approval rating ahead of the 1964 election campaign. Kennedy's entourage anxiously wondered whether Jackie would be well received by Americans after recent events. Doubts were dispelled as soon as she stepped off Air Force One in San Antonio. Impeccably dressed, she immediately won over the Texans with her hesitant smile. During the visit she played the role of First Lady to perfection, deliberately keeping to the sidelines. Yet she still found herself center stage, as was made immediately clear during the party held in the Grand Ballroom of the Texas Hotel in Fort Worth. The President joked with those in attendance, saying into the microphone "Two years ago in Paris I introduced myself by saying I was the man who had accompanied Mrs. Kennedy. This trip to Texas is giving me the same feeling."

The Kennedys upon their arrival on Air Force One at the airport in San Antonio, Texas, on November 21, 1963.

The next day, November 22, was clear and windy, and they climbed into a midnight-blue Lincoln Continental convertible to wave and smile to the crowd. "I don't want the roof on the car, all the Texans need to see what a pretty girl Jackie is," Kennedy had ordered. Then he asked her to take off her sunglasses, to show everyone her face. "Darling, it is you they have come to see," he said. Jackie, in her elegant pink suit, was sitting next to her husband when the shots were fired, fatally wounding the President in the head. He was the victim, but the most iconic images of those tragic moments are of Jackie throwing herself over the trunk of the car (to assist a Secret Service agent to climb into the car to help JFK) in that strawberry pink suit with blue lapels, destined to become the most legendary piece of clothing in American history. It was a boiled-wool Chanel model, custom-made for the First Lady by the Chez Ninon boutique in Manhattan under license of the Parisian fashion house.

Above, the Lincoln convertible parades through the crowd in Dallas on November 22, 1963, minutes before John Fitzgerald Kennedy's assassination.

Left, Jackie in the famous strawberry-colored Chanel boiled-wool suit that she wore that day.

The fabric of the skirt was stained red in front of the horrified gaze of those present. Those tragic moments were captured, quite by accident, on the so-called "Zapruder film," 26 silent, grainy seconds that captured the crime of the century. Filmed by a tailor named Abraham Zapruder, it would become the most famous and studied amateur film of all time. One of the most poignant frames captures Jackie's desperation as she tries to protect her newly murdered husband with her body. She held him in her arms for the duration of the drive to Parkland Memorial Hospital.

The smiling Kennedys, moments before the shooting that would end an era.

Six minutes later, the car stopped at the entrance to the emergency room. When a nurse approached to lift her husband's head, Jackie pushed her away and wanted to do it herself. She continued to run beside the stretcher, clutching Jack's hand as doctors transported him to the operating theater. She was still holding it when they announced that there was nothing more to be done. She tried to take off her wedding ring, to put it on her husband's finger, but her white leather gloves were so soaked in blood that she had to ask a policeman to help her slip them off.

In the dramatic moments following the first shot, Jackie tried to save her husband. Shortly after this, he would be killed by a second bullet.

A few hours later, the coffin was loaded onto Air Force One, where new President Lyndon Johnson would be sworn in before takeoff. When she boarded, someone had placed a clean dress in Jackie's cabin to allow her to change. She had wiped her face clean, but refused to remove the blood-soaked suit: "I want everyone to see what they did to Jack." In the stuffy presidential booth, she watched, devastated, as the oath was administered to Johnson. Then she sat beside the coffin for the duration of the flight. The whole world watched her descend the steps of Air Force One on the arm of her brother-in-law Bobby, bewildered and somber.

Aboard Air Force One just before takeoff from Dallas, Jackie witnesses the swearing-in of Vice President Lyndon Johnson. She is still wearing the blood-stained pink suit.

Above, standing next to her brother-in-law Bobby Kennedy as she watches in dismay as the coffin with her husband's remains is transported to the airport in Washington.

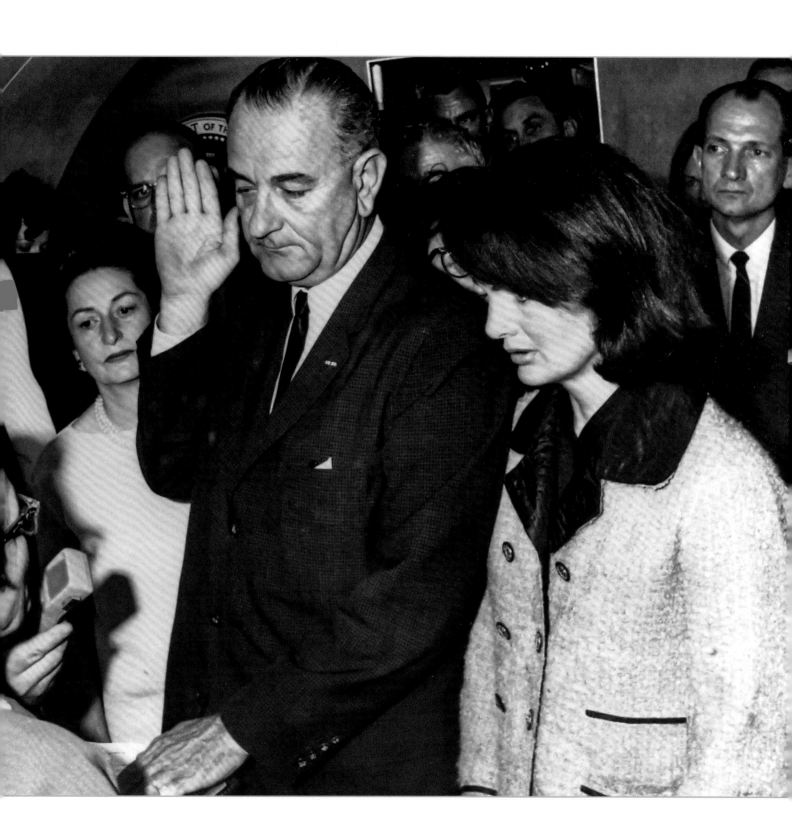

159

For the final farewell, she wanted the same ceremony for JFK that had been reserved for Abraham Lincoln. As the Navy band performed the *Funeral March on the Death of a Hero* from Beethoven's Third Symphony, she took the children, six-year-old Caroline and little John Jr., by the hand. He would turn three that very day, and in a gesture that would tear everyone apart, he brought his little hand to his forehead, attempting a military salute. The citizens waiting to file past the coffin displayed at the Capitol Rotunda formed a line more than five kilometers long to pay their last respects to the President. Jackie declared that she would follow the casket on foot throughout the funeral procession, and many heads of state did so with her, despite the danger of a new assassination attempt.

Above, the final salute to John Fitzgerald Kennedy's coffin, covered by the American flag.

On the opposite page, Jackie with children Caroline and John Jr. as they climb the steps of the Capitol in Washington on the day of the funeral, November 25, 1963.

New President Lyndon Johnson, Moscow Council of Ministers representative Anastas Mikojan, Prince Philip, Charles de Gaulle, and the other leaders of ninety-two countries walked beside the widow in the chill of that November day for the six blocks leading to the cathedral. A deafening silence surrounded the solemn procession, broken only by military drums and the sound of horseshoes. The funeral rites were officiated at St. Matthew's Cathedral, where Jackie knelt to kiss the American flag that enveloped her husband's coffin, before burial at Arlington National Cemetery.

Dressed in dignified mourning, her eyes welling with tears under the black veil that covered her face but failed to conceal her grief-hardened features, she was an illustrious and poignant figure. Her austere dignity and extraordinary self-control left an unforgettable impression, elevating her in the eyes of the public to a new role. She had become an icon. The London *Evening Standard* newspaper wrote, "Jacqueline Kennedy has given the American people the one thing they have always lacked: Majesty." The woman judged by many as delicate and frivolous proved to be the strongest of all. Bent over with grief, she devoted what energy she had left to cementing the legend of her husband's short presidency.

Along the route of the funeral procession, Jackie walks alongside her husband's brothers, Robert and Edward Kennedy.

A week after the funeral she contacted Theodore H. White, *Life* reporter and future Pulitzer Prize winner, to offer him an exclusive interview. Aware of the power of the media and her own charisma, Jackie won him over by drawing parallels between JFK's presidency and the mythical Camelot, King Arthur's court. She told White that Kennedy loved to listen to music at night on an old record player. His favorite song was a piece played by Richard Burton in a Broadway musical: it was called *Camelot*. And there was one line in particular, Jackie recounted, that he loved: "Don't let it be forgot, that once there was a spot, for one brief shining moment that was known as Camelot." The article came out on December 6, 1963, riding the emotional tide of the Dallas assassination and making the thousand days of Kennedy's presidency legendary.

In a poignant gesture, little John Jr. moved the world by raising his hand in a military salute as his father's casket passed by.

After that moment, Jackie tried to push on with her life, but she would endlessly relive the shock of the assassination during the sleepless and lonely nights that seemed to go on forever. No amount of vodka could restore her former peace of mind. "Like the Titanic, I sank into black, icy waters," she revealed to the press. In public she put on a brave face, but in private the heartbreak was intolerable. She put herself through torture by blaming herself for not having done enough to save her husband's life and seriously considered suicide. She was not just reacting to the grief, but to a much deeper wound. At the time, there was still no name for that kind of suffering. It was not named until a decade later, thanks to studies on Vietnam veterans who complained of sleep disturbances, obsessive thoughts and fleeing from any situation capable of reactivating unsettling memories. Jackie's experience reflected the same kind of distress, which today is called Post-Traumatic Stress Disorder. The mere idea of reliving the shock of gunshots was enough to throw her into a state of absolute terror. This happened even in the most unlikely places, such as at the theater. During an evening at the New York City Ballet, while watching with photographer Cecil Beaton the performance of choreographer George Balanchine, two gunshots resounded as part of the performance. They were enough to make her jump to her feet like a spring, ready to flee.

Her life had changed, forever. In early December, Jackie prepared to leave the White House, a painful step not only because of the terrible circumstances, but also because of the deep bond that united her to the residence, to whose splendor she had devoted so much energy. She wrote in her own handwriting the words to be affixed to the Lincoln Bedroom: "In this room lived John Fitzgerald Kennedy with his wife Jacqueline during the two years, ten months and two days he was President of the United States." Eleven days later, she left her Camelot forever. Initially she had chosen a brick house in the Georgetown neighborhood, where she asked the decorator to exactly replicate the bedrooms her children had lived in at the White House. Their own contentment came first, but regaining a semblance of normality was not easy. The sidewalk was besieged by reporters and onlookers trying to catch a glimpse of the widow and children through the windows. Cars, and even a few buses, were constantly parading past the entrance to the house. "There is only one thing I can do now in life: protect my children. They must be able to grow up without always thinking about their father's murder," she declared when she chose to leave Washington to start a new life in New York, away from bad memories and prying eyes. She longed to be able to walk around the city, take a cab and do all the normal things mothers with young children did. So she moved into an apartment on the fifteenth floor of 1040 Fifth Avenue.

Jackie chose to move with her children to New York City to start a new life. Here she is pictured with John Jr. in their new Manhattan apartment in September 1964.

The Ten Forty, as she called it, was furnished to her taste, with the Louis XVI desk on which Kennedy had signed the Nuclear Test Ban Treaty in 1963, a collection of seventeenth-century paintings of animals, and some Indian miniatures, as well as hundreds of books. First she took Caroline and John on a trip to Central Park, where no one seemed to recognize them; from that moment on, life slowly began to move again and Jackie found her smile. On weekends she loved to go horseback riding at equestrian clubs in New Jersey and spent whole days playing with the children at the Kennedys' estate in Hyannis Port, while in winter she took them skiing on the slopes of Aspen, Colorado, or Gstaad, Switzerland.

Above, Jackie with her children on a rowboat in the pond in Central Park, New York in 1964.

On the opposite page, she rides a horse with Caroline and John Jr. through the woods in search of some peace and serenity.

To escape from memories and reality, she traveled constantly. She flew to Argentina to spend the Easter vacations gallivanting on ranches, visited Andalusia with Prince Rainier and Princess Grace of Monaco, and spent a long vacation in Hawaii, which included hiking across volcanoes and nights of camping beneath the stars, which thrilled Caroline and John. She was seen in grainy pictures in the newspapers, captured by photographers as she walked down the street or when she appeared at a party on the arms of a string of different men. Particularly sensational was her much-talked-about trip to Cambodia with David Ormsby-Gore, the recently widowed British ambassador for the Kennedy presidency, and some spoke of a new engagement. But in reality, those moments away from the everyday for Jackie were nothing more than distractions, much-needed breaks to ease a suffering that had never subsided. Tributes, celebrations, and newspaper headlines continually reminded her of the tragedy, keeping her suspended in an impossible dilemma between the determination to forget what had happened and the duty to remember. It was a contained but devastating grief that was repeated four and a half years later when her brother-in-law Bobby was also killed.

Jackie in front of the ruins of Angkor, Cambodia, ambushed by photographers in November 1967.

Visiting Seville, Spain. Above, she rides a horse during the Sevillian féria *in a spotless Andalusian riding habit.*

On the left, she attends a bullfight wearing the traditional white lace mantilla.

Greeted by Queen Elizabeth II, Jackie and her children attended the opening of the John F. Kennedy Memorial in Runnymede, UK, on May 14, 1965.

In the opposite photo she listens to British Prime Minister Harold MacMillan deliver the official speech.

The father of eight children, he had also taken Jack's children under his wing since Jackie had been widowed, helping them cope with their grief. His and Jackie's shared sorrow had grown into a deep bond, and there were whispers that it had become something more. They spent whole days together and she supported him with all her influence when he decided to run for the presidency, leveraging the civil-rights struggle and the immense media exposure of the Kennedys. The dream was shattered once again by a gunshot that wounded Bobby as he was leaving the Ambassador Hotel in Los Angeles. Jackie rushed desperately to the hospital, but there was nothing more to be done. Present at Bobby's bedside were his wife Ethel and brother Ted, but it was Jackie who signed the authorization papers to pull the plug on the machines. Ever since her husband's death, she had been on edge, and Bobby's assassination only confirmed her fears. "They were killing the Kennedys, and I didn't want them to hurt my children. I wanted to escape, to be in a safe place," she would recount. She feared that she would be the next target, was obsessed by visions of her own death, and felt she needed someone to protect her and give her a sense of security. "Sometimes I think I will never be happy again," she confessed to friends. "I try, but I can't forget the pain. And when I feel happy, all I do is wait for it to come back." Overwhelmed by this storm, she chose to take the hand being extended to her by one of the most powerful men in the world.

Covered with a lace veil, Jackie tearfully attended the St. Patrick's Church funeral of her brother-in-law Bobby Kennedy, who was assassinated on June 6, 1968, during his presidential campaign.

The Lady of Skorpios (1968–1975)

Determined to start a new life, she married Greek shipowner Aristotle Onassis. From that moment on, she became "Jackie O" to everyone, a name destined to inspire a style, an era, and an iconic Gucci handbag.

The dark gangster glasses, the coiffed hair, the face perpetually shrouded in the smoke of a Montecristo cigar. Aristotle Onassis was nicknamed the "Golden Greek" because of his immense fortune. Thanks to a controversial and lightning-fast career, he rose from the poverty he suffered after the Greek-Turkish War of 1922 to boundless wealth generated by a hundred interlinked enterprises, including Olympic Airlines. After his divorce from his first wife, he seduced a host of famous women including Maria Callas, who was won over by his dark charm and generous gifts, but also by his cultured education. Onassis quoted Homer by heart and spoke eloquently in each of the five languages he was fluent in. Since Jackie had been his guest on the *Christina,* Onassis had telephoned her regularly and dined privately with her more than once. He had rushed to Washington for Kennedy's funeral, but it was not until after Bobby's assassination that he made up his mind to come forward, offering her love, protection, and safety, and manifesting his intentions with increasingly flamboyant gifts. Bracelets, tiaras, and earrings, accompanied by romantic notes, were delivered again and again to Jackie, who finally succumbed to his courtship. To seal their love, he gave her a magnificent 40-carat solitaire and signed a prenuptial agreement that would guarantee his future wife a princely annual income and a million-dollar settlement in the event of divorce. To that advantageous agreement she added an additional clause, that of not giving her husband more than three affairs a month.

Greek shipowner Aristotle Onassis.

Jackie Kennedy together with Aristotle Onassis, who left soprano Maria Callas for her.

Before the wedding, Jackie had wanted to introduce Onassis to her mother Janet. But Telis, as she affectionately called him, demanded the approval of the entire family, including the Kennedys. So, one June afternoon, she took him to Cape Cod, where he showed up with an expensive bracelet for matriarch Rose, to whom the couple announced their intention to marry. Jackie felt that marriage would be what Jack would have wanted for her under the circumstances. But few agreed. The news of the impending nuptials quickly went around the world, leaving everyone in disbelief. The press immediately lashed out against the union, hastily labeled as a deplorable exchange of interests between a greedy woman and an unscrupulous tycoon. It was the New York *Times*'s cutting headline that first gave voice to the general discontent: "Jack Kennedy Dies Today a Second Time." Soon after, other newspapers followed the wave of popular outrage, clamoring across their front pages "America Has Lost a Saint" and "Jackie Marries a Blank Check." Americans felt betrayed: the marriage was perceived as a veritable disgrace to the memory of their president, an affront to the entire nation and the American dream that the young and glamorous couple had represented. Jackie's global fame had turned into a trap. Her decision was considered an unacceptable affront, capable of wiping out in one clean sweep her status as an untouchable widow whom the press had always respected. Like everyone else, Maria Callas learned the news from the newspapers. Her romance with Onassis had filled the pages of magazines for years, enticing readers with tales of their tormented passion. Heartbroken, the soprano commented on the news with ostentatious nonchalance. "Jacqueline Bouvier Kennedy did well to give her children a grandfather," she declared, sarcastically pointing out the more-than-20-year age difference between the newlyweds. Equally dismayed was Lee Bouvier, the eternal second, who was Aristotle's longtime mistress and saw herself once again cast aside for her older sister. After all, Onassis had done his math right by betting on Jackie. To appear by her side symbolized reaching the pinnacle of power, and the outrage of the international press only underscored the magnitude of his feat. This wife, who was younger and taller than him, and far more famous, was his trophy. JFK's beautiful widow was the most famous woman in the world, made even more splendid by her tragic history. He compared her to a diamond: "Cold, angular contours, fiery and ardent beneath the surface." Jackie also seemed to have found what she needed. This man, whom many judged crass and vulgar, hid behind his exterior appearance a poetic sensibility and power that reassured her. For as long as she could remember, what she desperately sought was someone who could give her security, who would make her laugh again and tell her stories she had never heard. A man she could count on when she needed, but who would let her breathe when she wanted to be alone. At that moment, what she craved more than anything else was the sense of protection that the Kennedys could no longer give her. "I wanted to find a safe place and stay there," she declared. Her safe place was called Skorpios, the 400-acre Greek island that Onassis owned in the Ionian Sea.

It was there that they were married in the Orthodox Rite one October Sunday in 1968, in the presence of only 21 guests, amid clouds of incense and gold vestments. It rained all day on the cypress trees that surrounded the tiny 18th-century private chapel, lit only by candles. Jackie wore a short ivory dress with long sleeves finished with wide cuffs, a high collar, and lace accents. It was not a one-of-a-kind piece, but a fine haute couture dress by Valentino, chosen from one of the Italian designer's most famous collections, the White Collection, presented that very year. Discreet, modern, and feminine, Jackie's chosen wedding dress was an unprecedented success, and Valentino's Rome atelier was flooded with requests, selling more than 400 items in just a few days. Once again, Jackie launched a new fashion, that of second weddings celebrated in a white dress. It was an unusual choice for the time, since the color white, synonymous with purity, was considered suitable only for first weddings.

After the religious celebration, the guests boarded the *Christina* for the reception. Although the couple had asked the media to respect their privacy, a throng of journalists watched from afar, aboard fishing boats kept at a distance by an impressive security detail. The first images of the newlyweds and their families circulated immediately. Jackie had a tight smile on her lips, Onassis flaunted the swagger of a victor, 11-year-old Caroline displayed a tender, embarrassed air, while little John Jr. kept his eyes downcast throughout the ceremony. Representing the Kennedys were Pat and Jean, two of Jack's sisters. Also present that day were the tycoon's children, who were fiercely opposed to the wedding. Onassis had told them the news only a few days earlier. The eldest son Alexander hissed "Here we are, related to a courtesan," while his younger sister Christina would reserve an undying hatred for Jackie. She who at the time was still America's most famous and beloved widow, from that moment on became Jackie O. The world was split in two directions, between the admiration of those who appreciated her courage and the anger of those who argued that she had no right to rebuild her life. But not everyone was against the union. Friends and admirers celebrated the new couple from afar with affectionate messages, such as the telegram received from Paris that morning. "All the happiness in the world, magnificent Jacqueline. If only I were called Aristotle Onassis and not Maurice Chevalier." Father Cushing, who had been the spiritual adviser of the Kennedys, also publicly declared his support for Jackie. "I suggest leaving that woman alone. She has known tremendous sadness in life and deserves all the happiness she can get."

The Onassis wedding day on the Greek island of Skorpios, October 20, 1968. Jackie wears a white Valentino dress.

She really tried to be happy again. Photos of the couple taken at that time show them complicit and cheerful, with Jackie looking radiant sitting next to Onassis on the *Christina,* smiling in a Grecian shirt and green shawl at a tavern, stunning in a pair of sandals and a short cotton dress decorated with stars and crescent moons as she smiles at her husband, he in a dark suit. At that time, Emilio Pucci mini dresses, wide gypsy-style skirts, and cigarette pants had taken the place of elegant flared dresses and demure necklines in her wardrobe. It was a more informal and less demanding period, characterized by a different kind of elegance, which relied mainly on striking accessories like the Hermès scarves, the flat moccasins made in Italy that went down a storm in Manhattan boutiques, and the oversized sunglasses by French designer François Pinton. And a legendary handbag expressly dedicated to Jackie. It was shaped like a half-moon and had a golden lobster clasp and semi-polished leather inserts. It was marked with the Gucci signature and became an emblem of the era. In her honor, the Florentine fashion house decided to rename it "Jackie."

Jackie and Aristotle smiling at a bar table in Capri's Piazzetta, one of the stops on their Mediterranean cruise the summer after their wedding.

To the left, the couple strolls the streets of Capri amid a curious crowd.

Jackie's wardrobe during the years of her marriage to Onassis became less formal but remained utterly elegant. Accessories include a Gucci handbag renamed "Jackie" in her honor and oversized sunglasses.

Complementing the sophisticated simplicity of those looks was the gorgeous jewelry she continually received from her new husband, such as earrings with heart-shaped rubies or a ring with a stone so large she was forced to slip it off every time she had to use her hand to make a phone call. For her 40th birthday, Onassis gave her a pair of gold earrings studded with precious stones, designed by him in honor of the Apollo 11 Moon Landing a few days earlier. "Next year," he promised her, "if you're good, I'll give you the moon." In return, she bought him colorful ties to brighten his dark suits and composed with her own hands the albums in which she compiled the photographs taken under the Skorpios sun. During the weeks she spent in Greece, Onassis took care not only of her but also of her children. He spoiled them with expensive gifts, such as the six-meter boat christened with his name that Caroline received for her birthday, the pony for little John, and even the hot dogs he had delivered directly from Coney Island, shipping them on Olympic Airways flights from New York to Athens. He entertained the children for hours, telling them stories of Greek heroes and transporting them to the imaginative world of classical myths, and took them to explore the wild beauty of his scorpion-shaped island. He had spent a fortune turning it into a paradise, planting orchards, bougainvillea, jasmine, oleander, and the Mediterranean trees of Greek tradition: olive, fig, almond, cypress, and pine trees. Jackie spent entire days water-skiing and reading in the tranquility of the island. In the evenings she meditated on the beach, while little owls sacred to the goddess Athena flew in the golden light of dusk. Bit by bit, she immersed herself in the local culture, learned basic Greek and how to dance the sirtaki, and donned traditional costumes. To learn more about the history of her new homeland, she frequented intellectuals and scholars with her husband, then indulged in romantic walks with Onassis, who recited love poems to her in Greek. After revolutionizing the White House, she enjoyed transforming what would come to be known as the Pink House, the peach-colored, neoclassical-style mansion Onassis had built on the island. She filled it with furniture and works of art, unearthed by scouring the antique shops of Athens, and transformed it into a love nest.

Jackie celebrates her 40th birthday in Athens with Onassis. She wears a Pucci dress and earrings inspired by the Moon Landing received as a gift from her husband.

"The only routine with me is no routine at all."

Above and right, Jackie and Aristotle Onassis sailing on the Nile during a ten-day trip to Egypt in the spring of 1974.

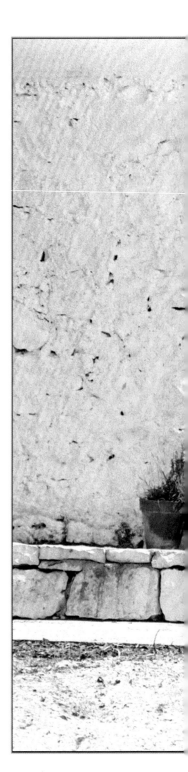

Relaxed and smiling, Jackie on a boat while vacationing on Skorpios in July 1975.

On the right, the private beach patio of the Pink House built by Onassis on the island, the furnishing of which Jackie personally oversaw.

The idyllic time, however, lasted the length of a summer. Arguments became more frequent as Jackie began spending long periods in New York, where Onassis rarely visited her. She had chosen to raise her children as Americans, and it was unthinkable to move them from their Manhattan schools. He resented his wife's long absences and was irritated by her wild spending. "Jackie O keeps filling her bottomless closets," gossiped women's magazines such as *Women's Wear Daily*. But what really caused a scandal were the pictures in which she appeared without those wonderful clothes, snapped by the prying lens of a paparazzo while she was sunbathing nude on a beach in Skorpios. The scandal erupted like a bombshell, and the *Hustler* magazine that published the shots sold two million copies. The episode only increased the tension for a couple now drifting apart. Aristotle and Maria Callas had started dating again and continued to see each other secretly in Paris. Soon, the paparazzi who followed them on their outings managed to catch them together, making the scandal public. When Jackie saw pictures of the lovers' secret dinner at Maxim's in the newspapers, she flew into a rage and considered divorce: she had endured enough betrayal and no longer wanted that kind of marriage. Yet in spite of everything, four years after the wedding, they were still close. Their anniversary was celebrated with a party in the champagne room of El Morocco in Manhattan, attended by some sixty guests, including members of the Kennedy family. Jackie wore a black top and a long white skirt, with a heavy Moroccan-style gold belt, posing smiling beside her husband. A few months later, a tragedy would shatter that apparent harmony forever.

Photographed on the streets of New York City, accompanying son John Jr. to school.

"Who is the woman who has best represented my style? Jackie Kennedy."

(Valentino)

With Italian fashion designer Valentino, during a benefit dinner at the Pierre Hotel in New York, June 7, 1976. On the right, she attends a fashion show with Eunice Kennedy.

Jackie's passion for fashion lasted a lifetime, as did her connection to France. She is pictured above, walking in Paris in the mid-1970s.

On the left, she visits the John F. Kennedy Center for the Performing Arts, immediately after attending a performance of Mass, *composer Leonard Bernstein's opera dedicated to the late president, whose statue stands behind them.*

Jackie on the arm of her son John Jr. at the funeral of her second husband Aristotle Onassis on the island of Skorpios, March 21, 1975.

To the left, she walks beside the shipowner's daughter, Christina Onassis.

On January 23, 1973, Alexander Onassis died aged 24 because his plane crashed in Athens. Aristotle aged suddenly. Despite his power, he had been unable to protect his son. Every night, he went to his grave with a bottle of ouzo and two glasses, one for himself, the other for his lost son, speaking to the tombstone as if Alexander were able to hear his weeping. Suddenly, the roles had been reversed. Now Jackie was the one who had to help him heal his wounds. The death seemed to have a domino effect, and shortly thereafter Athina, Onassis's first wife and mother of his children, also died. Soon afterward, the tycoon lost control of Olympic Airways and several business deals fell through. King Midas seemed to have lost his touch. Superstition haunted him, and he pondered ending his marriage to Jackie, who seemed to have attracted all sorts of adversity to him. He rewrote his own will, leaving all his assets to his daughter Christina, but guaranteeing Jackie a generous annual allowance.

He then summoned a lawyer to finalize the divorce, but he didn't get time to complete the paperwork. He was hospitalized in Paris when Jackie was warned that the situation was deteriorating, and on March 15, 1975, she received news in New York that Aristotle had died without her. She became a widow for the second time. On the day of the funeral, it was pouring with rain. The coffin, made of Skorpios walnut wood, was carried across the island to the chapel where they had been married. In the procession that followed, Jackie had been relegated to the back and was walking clinging to the arm of her son John Jr., hidden behind sunglasses and wrapped in a black raincoat, a stricken expression on her face. She made one single statement to the press about her controversial and troubled marriage: "Aristotle Onassis saved me at a time when my life was shrouded in shadow. He meant a great deal to me. He brought me into a world full of love and happiness."

The Empress of New York (1975–1994)

Endless charm and excessive wealth. Jackie's third life in Manhattan was all about culture. A successful editor and an influential public figure for the conservation of historical monuments, she was ready for new love.

"I believe that one of the best things we can do in life is to create a beautiful home, capable of housing future generations and preserving memories," Jackie said. She had made that dream come true, finding refuge away from the prying eyes of the world in an estate overlooking the sea on Martha's Vineyard, renamed Red Gate Farm. She had fallen in love with it from the first glance. It had a wonderful ocean view and was surrounded by meadows shaded by oaks and lodgepole pines that sheltered a small hunting lodge, the only structure on the estate. This unspoiled nature had captivated her, so she bought it and within three years remodeled it, building a villa, an outhouse, and a beautiful rose garden. In taming that wild landscape, Jackie was transported back to the Lasata, her idyllic childhood home and a mirage she had chased for a lifetime. She often left Manhattan to spend long periods in the utter comfort of the estate. Benches, baskets, and rustic furniture were arranged next to inviting upholstered sofas, and there were flowers in every corner of the house. Even when she was on vacation, she would get up at seven every morning and have a breakfast of half a bowl of cereal with skimmed milk, fruit, and coffee, served on a tray in bed. Then she would slip into a bathing suit and swimming cap to swim for two hours in the lake that bordered the property. On weekends she regularly visited the Kennedys in Hyannis Port, where she was overwhelmed by nostalgia. "I cannot remember Jack's voice clearly anymore," she confessed one day to her mother-in-law Rose, "but to this day I can't look at his pictures."

Smiling amid the Manhattan skyscrapers, Jackie disembarks from a trip on the Staten Island Ferry.

Jackie in the editorial office of Viking Press, the New York publishing house where she was hired as an editor.

On the left, she chooses with art director Bryan Holme the images to be published in the book In The Russian Style, *her first success.*

Her melancholy grew by the day, fueled by loneliness. At fourteen, John Jr. was attending Collegiate School on the Upper West Side, while seventeen-year-old Caroline was contemplating enrolling at Sotheby's Institute of Art in London. Now that her children didn't need her as much, Jackie felt lost. At forty-five, she was ready to move on. She needed to get out of the house and meet people who were doing interesting things, putting her energy and brilliant mind to good use. Instead of seeking the protection of powerful men, she decided that this time she would take her life into her own hands, using her intellectual potential to fulfill herself through work. It was a choice perfectly aligned with the changing attitudes toward the role of women under way in the 1970s. On a personal level, Jackie was certainly not a feminist. She had grown up in an environment where a girl was only expected to find a good husband. However, for the first time, she allowed herself the opportunity to really choose what her life would look like. It meant starting from scratch, but it was worth it. The press and the public greeted with disbelief the announcement that Viking Press would hire Jackie as an editor. It was her first job since her days as a correspondent for the *Times-Herald* in Washington. Some accused the editor-in-chief of hiring her for publicity; others thought it was just another of Jackie's whims. After all, she was now known more for her shopping tastes than her literary skills.

Jackie photographed in her office at Viking Press during an interview. Two years later, she would move to Doubleday. "I have a deep love for my work," she declared to reporters.

After securing a staggering amount of money through a settlement with Onassis's daughter, Jackie was undoubtedly one of the richest women in the world, and she certainly did not need the $200 weekly salary she was given for working four days a week as a publishing consultant. On the first day, a curious crowd was waiting for her to arrive at the entrance to Viking Press headquarters. Addressing the photographers and admirers, she quickly made it clear that she did not expect any preferential treatment. She was assigned a small room overlooking Madison Avenue and was quick to prove her intentions by showing up on time like all the other employees, waiting her turn in front of the photocopier, and making her own coffee. Her first major project was a tasteful publication entitled *In the Russian Style,* the fruit of a shared idea with doyenne of high fashion Diana Vreeland and released at the same time as the major exhibition on Russian costumes organized in 1976 by the Metropolitan Museum of Art in New York. Her name was printed prominently on the cover, and deservedly so: She had done a colossal amount of research among the archives, unearthing rare volumes and interviewing experts. Then she had flown to Moscow to help the exhibition's organizers secure the loan of some pieces considered essential, such as the green velvet upholstered sleigh that had belonged to Princess Elizabeth, daughter of Peter the Great and his wife Catherine. Jackie's trip to the Soviet Union reinforced the ties between East and West, somewhat bringing full circle the political détente between the two countries that was so desired by Kennedy. She was no longer the First Lady, but her status as "the most famous woman in the world" remained intact, as did her ability to attract attention. On the evening of the opening of the exhibition at the Met, the eyes of those in attendance were all on her, looking as elegant as ever in a tight, white strapless gown designed by Mary McFadden. As the air filled with Tchaikovsky's music and clouds of Chanel's Russian Leather perfume, Diana Vreeland introduced the exhibition, inviting everyone to appreciate Jackie's work and purchase her wonderful book that accompanied the exhibit. That success was an immensely gratifying moment that marked the beginning of a fruitful partnership with Viking. She became an expert in commissioning illustrated books and edited an anthology of Russian fairy tales and a collection of photographic portraits of Abraham Lincoln. Relations suddenly became strained when the publisher decided to publish the thriller *Shall We Tell the President,* a novel with a plot that eerily echoed the dynamics of the Kennedy assassinations. "When it was insinuated that I had something to do with the acquisition of the book and that I was unbothered by its publication, I felt I had to resign," Jackie announced in a public statement, resigning from Viking. A few months later, she accepted a new position at the Doubleday publishing house, where she would remain for the following sixteen years. Although a best-selling publisher, it allowed Jackie to work on a collection of niche books, with titles devoted to eighteenth-century women or photographs of gardens taken by Eugène Atget. Jackie also edited *Moonwalk,* Michael Jackson's autobiography released in 1988 and his biggest commercial success, which took four years to complete.

Although she stayed out of the spotlight during that period, her fame never stopped increasing, along with the world's admiration for her timeless style. This is evidenced by the series of blue-and-black silkscreens that Andy Warhol dedicated to her, taken from images obsessively reported in newspapers after the dramatic events in Dallas. United by their passion for art, they ended up becoming friends, and Jackie was invited several times to Warhol's famous estate in Montauk, where the Rolling Stones, John Lennon, Liz Taylor, Catherine Deneuve, Truman Capote, and Keith Haring were regular guests. Over time, Jackie learned to harness her tremendous notoriety, exercising her power to support the arts and sciences. It was also thanks to her intervention that a monument of such incalculable value as the Egyptian Temple of Dendur could be rescued from the waters of the Nile after the construction of the Aswan Dam, to be transported and reconstructed in a hall of the Metropolitan Museum of Art in New York.

Andy Warhol in his New York studio, with some silkscreens from the series dedicated to Jackie Kennedy.

Pictured behind Jackie is Grand Central Station, the historic New York City building that she pledged to preserve from demolition by participating in an awareness campaign.

Above, she participates in a 1978 Municipal Arts Society landmark protection rally.

Her sensitivity to the loss of culture also led her to worry about the disappearance of historic corners of Manhattan, such as Grand Central Station, in place of which a fifty-five-story commercial tower designed by Marcel Breuer was scheduled to be built. For once, instead of evading the press, Jackie was eager to show herself and make her voice heard. "The station is a beautiful building. It outrages me to think that it could be replaced by steel and glass," she said in front of hundreds of like-minded activists. She traveled with them by train from New York to Washington, D.C., on April 16, 1978, to raise awareness about the protection of historic monuments. The Landmark Express, as it was renamed, had many famous personalities on board, but none caught the attention of the press quite like Jackie. After the Supreme Court ruled in favor of preserving Grand Central Station with protected landmark status, Jackie lent her presence to other campaigns, such as preventing the demolition of Lever House, an iconic landmark; stopping the construction of an office complex over St. Bartholomew's Church; and forcing a developer to lower the height of a planned new complex on Columbus Circle.

She had loved New York ever since she chose to settle in Manhattan so many years earlier, hoping that the anonymity of a bustling metropolis would offer her room to breathe, a place to be herself. In that immense city she convinced herself that she could escape her endless fame and was confident that a reclusive lifestyle would eventually ward off the press. But it did not. She was constantly besieged by photographers, who were perpetually on the lookout for front-page shots. The most persistent was a freelancer from the Bronx, Ron Galella. He would lurk for hours, suddenly emerging with his camera to capture the bewilderment on people's faces. And to snap that moment, he was willing to do anything. He would pop up in disguise with a wig and fake mustache so as not to be recognized, following Jackie to clubs, restaurants, theaters, and stores. He was obsessed with his subject, so much so that she began to feel threatened. She had no way of predicting when he would surge with his camera, but she was certain it would happen and there was nothing she could do to prevent it. The aesthetic of Galella's images specificaly emphasized Jackie's vulnerability and the sense of helplessness she felt in front of his lens, triggering memories and feelings related to Kennedy's assassination and the trauma she endured. In 1970 she sued him, obtaining a restraining order to which Galella responded by suing her for "interference with the exercise of his lawful occupation." She accused him in turn of harassment and invasion of privacy, but it took her three years to obtain another restraining order. Sitting on the witness stand, in a courtroom overflowing with onlookers lined up since dawn, she declared her discomfort with Galella's constant presence, persuading the judge to order the photographer to stay at least a 50-yard distance from her and a 75-yard distance from her children.

Jackie on the streets of Manhattan, pursued by paparazzo Ron Galella. She will obtain a restraining order against the photographer to protect her privacy and that of her children.

During that period, images taken by Galella, and by dozens of other reporters, captured the evolution of Jackie's style, which, in the early 1980s, underwent yet another transformation. With the Givenchy and Cassini eras passed, she handed over the role of trusted friend and stylist to Carolina Herrera. Jackie's looks, even when she was well into her fifties, remained a reliable benchmark for every woman. In New York she preferred to wear inconspicuous colors and patterns, especially to work. She often wore black turtleneck sweaters, masculine pants, and an open trench coat, the loose-fitting androgynous outerwear in line with fashion trends. For beach vacations, her favorite clothing became flowing calf-length skirts, lightweight sheath dresses, and palazzo pajamas, which she could wear with a unique grace. She wore very subtle makeup and, as always, knew how to enhance her outfit with the right accessories: the shiny black leather shoulder bag, matching Mary Jane shoes, a Pucci scarf over her head, and the legendary oversized round-rimmed glasses. On her wrist she almost always wore the Cartier Tank watch given to her by her brother-in-law Stanislaw Radziwill, her sister Lee's second husband.

Jackie's style in the mid-1970s followed the trend of sleek lines and androgynous clothing, such as the trench coat. Once again, it was the accessories that made the difference. On the left, note the Gucci handbag and oversized sunglasses.

Above, her Tank watch by Cartier, a gift from her brother-in-law Stanislaw Radziwill, with the dedication "Stas to Jackie, 23 Feb. 63" engraved on the back.

Her romantic pursuits also reflected this new way of life. After a series of real or alleged lovers, more or less famous, she chose to live a quiet romance with Maurice Tempelsman, a very wealthy jewelry merchant different from the men she had been attracted to in the past. Stocky and mature, he was still married to the mother of his three children when they met. Born in Belgium the same year as Jackie, he had grown up in a Jewish family that fled to the United States just before World War II. He had first crossed paths with Jackie at the White House during a Kennedy state dinner in 1961, and they had met again when he became her financial adviser after Onassis's death. Over time, the elegant but shy man's unobtrusive presence at Jackie's side became increasingly noticeable on social outings, when he accompanied her to gala dinners or exhibition openings. They both loved art and ballet, antiques and literature, sometimes indulging in the habit of conversing in French, a language they both loved and spoke fluently. Heedless of onlookers and photographers, they took long walks in verdant Central Park, living in separate houses. When Tempelsman obtained a divorce from his wife, he took up residence in a hotel near Jackie, then moved into her apartment at Ten Forty. "The first time, you marry for love, the second for money, and the third for companionship," she had let slip in an interview. Although they never married, Jackie found in that new love a sense of peace she had spent a lifetime searching for.

Jacqueline Bouvier Kennedy Onassis photographed with Maurice Tempelsman at the entrance to a party at the New York Public Library in November 1982.

Epilogue

After a life in the limelight, Jacqueline Bouvier Kennedy Onassis died at the age of sixty-four. She left the world with the extraordinary image of a woman capable of reinventing her life and style over and over, while always remaining true to herself.

After Kennedy's assassination, Jackie had agreed to return to the White House only once, in 1971, to attend the unveiling of their official portraits. In the years that followed, she stayed away from politics forever, focusing on her professional role and the education of her children. She saw both of them graduate from law school and emotionally witnessed Caroline's wedding to Edwin Schlossberg, the CEO of a New York company that designed museum exhibits, celebrated in a ceremony at the small church of Our Lady of Victory, a few miles from the Kennedys' property. She became grandmother to three grandchildren, Rose, Tatiana, and John. She proudly watched her son John Jr. deliver his first speech at the 1988 Democratic National Convention in Atlanta, then admired him on the cover of *People,* which named him "the sexiest man alive." He would become a young entrepreneur with a striking physique and an ominous fate, like many Kennedys before him. Jackie would not live long enough to meet the woman he would marry, Carolyn Bessette, who was beautiful, elegant, and incredibly similar in style to Jackie herself.

It wasn't until she reached her sixties that she came to accept the curious stares of the people around her and the insinuations continually directed at her by newspapers, commenting on her every move. Still, no one had the vaguest idea what she had to endure in the most hidden corners of her heart. "Sometimes I don't understand why they go out of their way to hurt me," she said of her critics. Those judgments, though, no longer mattered to her. She had made peace with the idea of being a celebrity and with the daily siege of the press. The feeling of being encircled and misunderstood that had always haunted her ceased to frighten her. Paraphrasing Eleanor Roosevelt, she argued convincingly that "No one can humiliate me without my consent." The wrinkles that furrowed her face did not affect her beauty or that Mona Lisa smile. Flawless on every occasion, she continued to sport an enviable figure and smoke two packs of cigarettes a day, a vice that, incredibly, she had always managed to hide from the public. All her life she had been proud of her slim, athletic figure, consistently maintained through swimming, running, and proper nutrition. That physical integrity, cultivated with such care, was her stronghold. That is why she was devastated when, at age sixty-four, she was diagnosed with non-Hodgkin's Lymphoma. Once again, just like in Dallas, she was forced to confront the randomness of tragedy. She had believed she could control her fate more than she actually could, and discovered herself vulnerable while the world continued to see her in her absolute splendor. "They will get used to seeing me this other way," she told her children after undergoing a round of chemotherapy. "If my hair falls out, I'll wear a wig." At that time, the press were kept at a distance. The few stolen shots still show Jackie as extraordinarily attractive, as if her charm was simply immune to any attack, and her energy remained intact. After all, she had said from a very young age: "I want to live my life, not record it." She also repeated this in one of her last interviews. To reporters who asked her "How has your life been, Mrs. Bouvier?" she replied, with a cold gleam in her eyes, "Interesting."

In the months that followed her diagnosis, the cancer did not take long to spread, and Jackie decided to suspend treatment to spend what time she had left in her comfortable Manhattan apartment at 1040 Fifth Avenue. She instructed her attorneys to prepare a living will in which she asked her children to refrain from any medical intervention to keep her alive artificially. She wished to remain lucid until the very end and did not want to stop working. She had manuscripts delivered to her home, which she would concentrate on reading for hours. Maurice Tempelsman stayed by her side each and every moment, holding her hand. One Sunday in May, he accompanied Jackie on a final walk through Central Park, around the body of water that she so loved and which the city would rename after her to honor her memory. Four days later, she was gone forever. It was May 19, 1994. It was John Jr. who made the announcement to the newspapers: "She passed on surrounded by friends, family, books, and the things she loved. She did it in her own way and on her own terms. And we all feel lucky for that." Soon after, a host of admirers gathered in front of Ten Forty, depositing armfuls of flowers in Jackie's memory. The funeral was worthy of a queen. The coffin, covered with ferns and lilies of the valley, was carried down Park Avenue surrounded on both sides by an emotional crowd, to the 19th-century Church of St. Ignatius Loyola. There were hundreds of dignitaries present, in front of whom John Jr. and Caroline poignantly shared several readings that reflected Jackie's passion for literature.

The First Lady who had first exalted and then outraged America was buried in Arlington Cemetery next to her husband's grave. Watching over them forever is the eternal flame that Jackie herself had lit on the hill many years before. Across the river, the bells of the Washington National Cathedral rang sixty-four chimes, one for each year of her life. On her tombstone, in addition to the dates of her birth and death, are the words "Jacqueline Bouvier Kennedy Onassis. Her three souls, her three lives."

"Every moment one lives is different from the other. The good, the bad, hardship, the joy, the tragedy, love, and happiness are all interwoven into one single, indescribable whole that is called life."

Jackie at the helm during a boat trip.

Author

Chiara Pasqualetti Johnson. A journalist from Milan with a degree in History of Art, she writes about travel, art, and lifestyle for leading Italian magazines. She is the author of several women's biographies published by White Star, including *The Most Influential Women of Our Time* (2018), translated into fourteen languages; *Coco Chanel: A Revolutionary Woman* (2020), a best seller with six international editions; *Chanel N°5: The Perfume of a Century* (2021), dedicated to the world's most famous perfume; *Girls Rule: A Collection of Women Who Defied Social Standards* (2022); and *Our Fair Lady: Audrey Hepburn's Life in Pictures* (2022). In 2021 she was named by Forbes Italy as one of the 100 Wonder Women of the Year, a list of successful women united by their strong leadership and creativity.

Bibliography

JFK, Fredrik Logevall, Random House, 2020 • *The Kennedy Heirs: John, Caroline, and the New Generation,* J. Randy Taraborrelli, St. Martin's Press, 2019 • *Jackie, Janet & Lee,* J. Randy Taraborrelli, St. Martin's Press, 2018 • *The Fabulous Bouvier Sisters,* Sam Kashner, Harper, 2018 • *Jackie and Cassini: A Fashion Love Affair,* Lauren Marino, Running Press, 2016 • *Jacqueline Bouvier Kennedy Onassis: The Untold Story,* Barbara Leaming, St. Martin's Griffin, 2015 • *Jack Kennedy: Elusive Hero,* Chris Matthews, Simon & Schuster, 2012 • *Jackie after O,* Tina Cassidy, Harper, 2012 • *Jackie Kennedy,* Yann-Brice Dherbier, Pierre-Henri Verlhac, White Star, 2012 • *Jackie as Editor: The Literary Life of Jacqueline Kennedy Onassis,* Greg Lawrence, Thomas Dunne Books, 2011 • *Jacqueline Kennedy: Historic Conversations on Life with John F. Kennedy,* Michael Beschloss, Hyperion, 2011 • *The Eloquent Jacqueline Kennedy Onassis: A Portrait in Her Own Words,* Bill Adler, William Morrow, 2004 • *Ask Not,* Thurston Clarke, Henry Holt and Company, 2004 • *Jackie Style,* Pamela Clarke Keogh, It Books, 2001 • *Jacqueline Kennedy: The White House Years,* Hamish Bowles, Bulfinch Press, 2001 • *America's Queen,* Sarah Bradford, Penguin Books, 2000 • *Happy Times,* Lee Radziwill, Assouline, 2000 • *Jackie After Jack: Portrait of the Lady,* Christopher Andersen, William Morrow, 1998 • *In the Kennedy Style: Magical Evenings in the Kennedy White House,* Letitia Baldrige, René Verdon, Doubleday, 1998 • *As We Remember Her: Jacqueline Kennedy Onassis in the Words of Her Family and Friends,* Carl Sferrazza Antony, HarperCollins, 1997 • *A Woman Named Jackie,* David Heyman, Penguin, 1995 • *One Special Summer,* Jacqueline Lee Bouvier, Delacorte Press, 1974 • *The Bouviers: Portrait of an American Family,* John H. Davis, Farrar, Straus & Giroux, 1969

Photo Credits

WS White Star Publishers® is a registered trademark property of White Star s.r.l.

© 2023 White Star s.r.l.
Piazzale Luigi Cadorna, 6
20123 Milan, Italy
www.whitestar.it

Translation: Stephanie Williamson – Editing: Phillip Gaskill

ISBN 978-88-544-2001-4
1 2 3 4 5 6 27 26 25 24 23

Printed in Italy by Rotolito S.p.A. - Seggiano di Pioltello (MI)